LEARNING
TO LET GO

D0273225

To Gail Trussler

whose friendship I value immensely,

whose thinking and writing has illuminated my understanding,

and whose help with this book has been invaluable.

LEARNING TO LET GO

MAKING THE TRANSITION INTO RESIDENTIAL CARE

PENELOPE WILCOCK

LION

Copyright © 2010 Penelope Wilcock
This edition copyright © 2010 Lion Hudson

The author asserts the moral right
to be identified as the author of this work

A Lion Book
an imprint of
Lion Hudson plc
Wilkinson House, Jordan Hill Road,
Oxford OX2 8DR, England
www.lionhudson.com

ISBN 978 0 7459 5398 4

Distributed by:
UK: Marston Book Services, PO Box 269, Abingdon, Oxon, OX14 4YN
USA: Trafalgar Square Publishing, 814 N. Franklin Street, Chicago, IL 60610
USA Christian Market: Kregel Publications, PO Box 2607, Grand Rapids,
MI 49501

First edition 2010
10 9 8 7 6 5 4 3 2 1 0

All rights reserved

This book has been printed on paper and board independently certified
as having been produced from sustainable forests.

A catalogue record for this book is available
from the

Typeset in 11/15 Aldine 721 BT
Printed and bound in Great Britain , Somerset

HOUNSLOW LIBRARIES	
FEL	
C0000 002 468 979	
Askews	31-Mar-2010
362.61	£7.99

Contents

Foreword 6

Introduction 8

Chapter 1   Starting to think about a care home   12

Chapter 2   Families and friends   36

Chapter 3   Affirming people as unique individuals   66

Chapter 4   The people and the place   96

Chapter 5   Learning to let go begins now   125

Notes   155

Appendix of useful contacts and   156
starting points

Foreword

How I wish I'd had this book a couple of years ago! That's when the physical and mental health of my own much-loved mum deteriorated to the degree that it became clear that living in our home as part of our family was no longer safe for her – or possible for us. It was a heartbreaking decision in which so many emotions came into play. For us, there was a huge sense of guilt that perhaps we could – and *should* – have been able to do more. I can't get out of my mind, even now, the expression of pleading on her face on the many occasions she'd made me promise that I'd never "let them put her in a home" – and because of that promise, I still feel a huge sense of betrayal that, with all the love in the world, I eventually allowed that dreaded outcome to happen. For her, there came the realization that this would almost certainly be the last move she ever made. She was tired, as if she'd run out of puff at the end of life's long race – but she was not emotionally ready to hang up her boots. She was confused and tearful one day, then positive and as bright as a button the next. And in that cameo of our own family life, I guess I've touched on the experience of many others who, like me, have longed for a book just like this to be written.

Penny Wilcock comes to the situation from so many angles because she's been a chaplain in a hospice, a care assistant for the terminally or chronically sick, and a pastor in churches where the congregation was mostly in the older age group. She has listened, watched, observed, and finally managed to draw up some sensitive, empathetic, and constructive thoughts on the complex set of emotions and circumstances which bring individuals and families to the reality that either they, or perhaps one of their parents, need to consider moving into sheltered or residential care. She recognizes the impact on the family, the fear on all sides, the need for trust and boundaries, respect and dignity. She touches on grief, loss, relief, love, opportunity, loneliness, friendship, the future – and so much more. She looks at the role of care staff and the importance of their kindness, patience, and ability to see the precious individual within an ageing body. And she affirms the intricate, wondrous mix of mind, body, and soul that is the miracle of each and every human being.

You can read this book on so many levels – as a textbook packed full of good and practical ideas; as a comfort to reassure you that you're not alone in this challenging, emotional situation; and last, quite simply, as a really good "read" that will keep you glued from page to page. This is one book you won't *want* to let go.

Pam Rhodes
Songs of Praise
BBC Television

Introduction

Care homes fall into two principal categories: residential care and nursing care. Residential care is for clients who are relatively able, but in need of support in daily living. It is the same level of care and help that a relative or friend looking after a vulnerable person would offer. Staff in a residential care home can help with washing, dressing, at meal times, with personal hygiene and going to the toilet. In some residential care homes, help in gaining skills that increase independence may be offered.

Nursing homes offer 24-hour nursing care by trained nursing staff (nurses and care staff). A nursing home will have a qualified doctor or nurse overseeing the care offered, and there will always be nursing staff as well as care staff on duty. Nursing care is for clients who need much more support, so people often need to move from residential to nursing care if their condition deteriorates – their move to the residential home isn't necessarily for life.

In both residential care homes and nursing homes, some of the residents will have left their homes permanently – sold them and ended their time as an independent householder. Others will have been encouraged by relatives to come into a care home – "just for a while", "until you feel better", "while we get things sorted out", "to see how you go on" – and may be cherishing a hope of returning home that those around them cannot share. Others again may come into a care home for respite care. Respite clients need care temporarily – if their carer at home is ill or on holiday, if they need a period of care following surgery, or if their spouse dies and they are temporarily unable to cope, for instance. A client may go in for respite care and then end up having to stay. Respite clients often do not know how long their stay will be. They may even have been taken against their will if their house was seen as unfit to live in – this happens when people's homes are dirty and untidy enough to be a health and safety hazard, or are found to have an infestation problem, for example. Often new clients are confused and disoriented or angry, because they don't want to be there and they don't understand why they've been taken from their home.

So, it is important to remember that people have different levels of need and different or uncertain patterns of residential stay. But, in every case, people going into a care home are facing a level of change in their lives that will affect them emotionally and spiritually. Even those who go in temporarily, for respite care, are on a difficult journey, requiring soul work as well as practical support. We must acknowledge the magnitude of the emotional and psychological adjustment that confronts someone who must now seek this level of support in everyday living. Those leaving home for the last time to enter residential care accommodation, because of increasing frailty or debilitating illness, should be offered understanding and help to face this most difficult of journeys.

If we do this – if we permit the grief and bewilderment, the bitter losses of dignity, identity, and comforting memory to be addressed – then we strengthen the likelihood of enabling this last stretch of the journey (however long or short it may be) to be moved from the category of "dying" to that of "living", for those leaving their own homes knowingly for the last time.

For those coping with multiple changes and uncertain futures, or seeking respite care for reasons of trauma, frailty, or vulnerability, help in adjusting to a new environment is strengthening and reassuring, assisting the process of healing and re-establishing personal equilibrium in someone whose context has lost stability.

There is no way for us to help others engage with this process without getting to grips with it first in our own lives and souls. The best pastoral help arises from authenticity, understanding, and the earthiness of compassion in a friend who knows the score.

So this is not a book about "them" but about "us". Until "they" become "us", none of our arm's-length pastoral assistance, however kindly meant, will make a difference.

Who will need to consider these issues and read this book? It may be that people who have reason to believe they will soon be unable to manage in their own homes are looking for something to help them consider the issues as they order their thoughts. There may be some who are beginning to find the burden of caring for a relative at home overwhelming and will find some reading helpful as they think through the implications of alternatives. Care staff looking at the spiritual care aspect of their role may find their thinking stimulated. Church pastors or those newly appointed as chaplains (whether lay or ordained) may find useful pastoral pointers here, and those who are working, or beginning to work, as volunteers in a care home chaplaincy team may also find food for thought in this book.

I should explain at the outset that this book is not designed to address a particular one of the variety of care contexts (residential, nursing, respite, permanent, assessment), and it is not written for a particular one of the possible readership groups (potential residents, carers at home, care staff, or chaplains and their volunteers). What is addressed here is the work that must be done to support people spiritually and emotionally as they face the transition from living in their own homes to living in a care home. I hope it will be helpful to the individuals themselves, to all those involved in their support, and to any one of us – for all of us are likely at some time in our lives to find this material of relevance.

Often in the course of the book, mention is made of chaplaincy teams who may visit and offer support. By no means all residential care homes or nursing homes will have a chaplain or associated team of volunteers, but some do, and all could. A chaplaincy team will add valuable support and enrichment. If you are reading this and wondering why there is none in the care home you are connected with, perhaps you could be instrumental in the formation of a chaplaincy group.

CHAPTER 1

Starting to think about a care home

In 2007, a Lancashire County Council research survey[1] returned statistics that showed the top concern for people over sixty-five to be the fear of losing independence. The research was conducted among people all aged over forty-five, showing that where worries about money most affected people up to fifty-five, after that anxiety focused on loss of independence.

Sixty-two per cent were afraid of not being able to get out and about; 52 per cent said they did not want to become dependent on others; and 48 per cent were afraid of having to leave their homes.

Of the 1,700 people surveyed, 69 per cent cited being able to stay in their own homes as the most important aspect for a happy life in old age.

The only thing that surprises me is that the percentage was not even higher.

"Going into care" is a matter of dread for many, many elderly or infirm people, or others whose needs makes it hard for them to be safe living in their own homes.

A neighbour of mine, in her eighties, recently made the transition from living alone in her large semi-detached villa to residential care. She was desperately lonely, she had had many falls, and she could not go out alone or get upstairs. She had two sons, one living abroad but making frequent trips home to see her, the other doing all he could to put together a care package that would support her adequately at home. She was loved, she had friends, but the time came when she needed someone on hand round the clock. It was very evident that she could no longer manage, and yet, in those difficult weeks and months as her family monitored her situation, assessing what could be done to get things right for her, a friend and frequent visitor to her home whispered to me, eyes big with drama and voice laden with emotion, "She don't want her sons to know how bad she is, because she's frightened they'll have her put away!"

To say that "going into care" has a bad press would be an understatement of monumental inadequacy. This book is about what we might do to make that transition easier: the acknowledgment of how much is lost, the rebuilding of a sense of self, the issues that should be considered in helping people to accept dependency without losing the ability to be happy.

Our task will be to look steadily at how much we ask of people when they must give up their homes for the last time. So there will be much said about trauma, sadness, and bereavement.

We will take a very careful look at what every one of us reading these pages might do to make ready for the time when "we" morph into "them" and become in our own turn the frail, the incontinent, the bent, slow souls with the ulcerated legs, going along slowly with the aid of a walking frame to the postbox at the corner. What attitudes, what habits of mind and life, could be the gift of today to tomorrow?

But right here at the outset, before we work through the difficult issues to be addressed and steadily faced, let's not forget that – however much they might have dreaded making the transition – lots and lots of people have a really nice time in residential care.

The right place

The key to a successful outcome is, of course, finding the right place. That achieved, it can be the beginning of a new lease of life not only for the individual concerned but for all those who bore the responsibility for their care at home as well.

A friend of mine whose mother had Alzheimer's disease talked to me about the impossibility of giving her mother the care she needed – precisely because she *was* her mother. A mother–daughter relationship is often hierarchical – mother's wishes are to be respected, her preferences observed; her daughter is to treat her with due deference. Mother gives advice and often laments aloud the failure of the younger generation to do anything (from table manners to international banking) properly. When the time comes that her daughter must tell her in no uncertain terms to change her knickers, and insists on going through the fridge or tracking down that very iffy smell emanating from the wardrobe, the balance of the relationship is badly threatened. Let battle commence!

When my friend's mother "went into care", the focus was all on the safety and supervision of the mother. The bonus never even considered beforehand was that, in the short time left before her mother descended into infirmity, the two of them had their friendship back again. My friend became the welcome visitor bringing special treats and the promise of outings, the person who stayed to chat and share a cup of tea, instead of the evil witch who humiliated her own mother by ferreting out soiled linen and mouldy corned beef.

When they "go into care", people who dared not venture much past their kitchen doorstep, whose gardens resemble nothing so much as virgin rainforest with a strong emphasis on buddleia, can once again sit out in the June sunshine and enjoy a cup of tea surrounded by well-kept roses.

People whose leisure options extended to television or sitting quietly find Scrabble partners, discussion groups, in-house communion services, and a visiting library when they "go into care".

Having someone to wash your hair, the possibility of eating freshly cooked vegetables, and someone else to lug that heavy vacuum cleaner around can all be a tremendous relief.

With the ascendency of family-friendly software from innovators like Nintendo, some residential care homes are able to put their televisions to good use in offering regular Wii Fit sessions to encourage residents to set their own levels in staying supple and active, and connected in to the developments of modern leisure pursuits.

Such a reality is nothing to dread!

It's important to make the distinction between a transition that is difficult because it is a move from something desirable to something undesirable, and something that is a positive move but is challenging because thresholds and transitions always are. So let's be clear that we are not here joining forces with my neighbour's wild-eyed friend, shaking our heads in mute disgust that people must be "put away". We are saying that the practical, good, helpful, life-enhancing option of residential care, even while it offers so much to individuals and their families, still requires courage, still asks a great deal, and still calls for imaginative and sensitive pastoral support.

When it comes to searching out the right residential care home, the variables and possibilities are almost endless. The choice is a very individual one. Even what might at first seem to be obviously limiting factors – money, for example – may not necessarily be so. Some residential accommodation of a very rough-and-ready, cheap-and-cheerful ambience might suit some people better than a rarefied and plush or clinical atmosphere of a more expensive home offering "better" facilities.

Some residential care homes offer a programme of

opportunities to make friends and keep active – music and movement classes, singalongs and coach trips – whereas others may offer a calm and dignified atmosphere with a beautiful garden to enjoy. One prospective resident may prioritize the privacy of an en suite bathroom, whereas another may be content with shared facilities or a commode.

It is a matter of taking the time to consider what really matters to the person who is going to live there. It is also worth enquiring among people who work locally as care assistants. Very often, among elderly populations the reputation of a care home can relate to what it used to be like ten years ago, when you need to know what it is like today. What do the agency nurses and carers think?

"How on earth do I find out that?" you may be wondering. Care assistants are not a well-paid workforce. I should think many of them keep an eye on Freecycle, the website where unwanted household items are given away free. A question posted on the café section noticeboard might draw a response. Many faith communities take the care of their elderly seriously, so enquiring at a church or mosque or gurdwara might give some helpful feedback.

"Is the food nice?" is not the sort of question that will tell you what you need to know. Nor is "Are the staff kind?" It depends what kind of food you like, and the staff may be kind to your friend's mother, but not necessarily to yours. Your friend's mother might be a real poppet whereas yours may be an absolute witch. But having a look at the way the rooms are organized and what facilities for receiving visitors are offered, enquiring about moving and lifting policies, the programme of in-service training given for care assistants as well as nurses, the ratio of staff to residents, and the levels of MRSA infection in the place might yield a little more information.

Inspection reports giving very helpful information are published online, but even then some important details can be missed. Only two out of three stars were given to one of the most loving care homes I know – a place where the manager/proprietor instigated the wonderful custom of having the funerals of residents take place there within the sitting room of the home. The coffin is brought in and placed on trestles in the conservatory, against a backdrop of the beautiful garden beyond; the organist brings her keyboard, and all the residents and staff are able to attend. No one is left out because they are too poorly or on duty that day – everyone is included. The residents in this care home were too frail in health for it to be practical to consider taking any significant number of them out to the funeral, and some of the care staff would inevitably have to stay behind to look after those who could not go. When you consider how integral a part of that community of staff and residents each resident becomes, it begins to feel very fractured and sad that most funerals of residents could normally include only a small delegation of one or two staff members to represent the home, and usually none of the other residents. A care home that would pioneer so sensitive and imaginative an initiative has my attention immediately.

A visiting inspector may not ask the questions that would turn up such information, so inspection reports are most useful in conjunction with personal acquaintance or recommendation from a trusted friend. Having said this, published inspection reports provide an immensely helpful resource for anyone beginning to investigate the residential care possibilities in their local area, and may include information about where and how to obtain a care assessment and help with finance.

In the appendix at the back of the book, you will find a list of useful websites and organizations offering this sort of practical help, information, and advice.

When the time has come to leave one's own home and find residential care accommodation, there may be a sense of relief: struggling on with insufficient help can leave us feeling desperate, vulnerable, and afraid. Even so, all change brings challenges, and it is wise to take the time to think through the emotional impact of such big changes, however welcome and necessary they may be. It is important, too, to consider and establish what are the hopes, priorities, and expectations of the person "going into care", doing a reality check on those, and forming a vision for a way forward that is both feasible and desirable.

Grief at what is lost

Over a number of years employed as a church pastor, meeting with people who were dealing with life's big issues – birth, marriage, sickness, death, family trouble – I have often seen people shed tears and express grief and sorrow, but not very often in nursing homes. This seems odd to me. When it is plain to see how fiercely people cling to their homes, memories, and possessions, would they not weep to leave them?

If I were a widow living in a little bungalow that my husband (God rest his soul) had built with his own hands, and where I had planted the garden, with an old tabby cat lying by the ashes of the fire, and the paintings and sculptures of my children displayed on the walls and shelves, I should weep to leave that place. If I were leaving the home where the plaster bore the pencil marks of the heights of my children as they grew, the place where my youngest was born one stormy June morning, the kitchen where the family gathered every day to eat the nourishing one-pot meals where a tiny bit of meat was augmented by beans and carrots and potatoes and barley until it fed us all, I would weep inconsolably. If I were that widow saying goodbye to my Norfolk chair and my Orkney chair (the one that came from my mother) and the kelims I picked up at the flea market, and the olive tree I'd been growing in a pot on the terrace for twenty-four years, and the china tea-service that came from my great-grandmother, and the canteen of cutlery that my husband's parents had for a wedding present, I would weep and weep as my heart broke over many months.

I remember once seeing a mother go to the rescue of her little girl who had fallen and grazed her knee. The child was horrified by the trickle of blood, and as she comforted her, the mother said, "It's good for it to bleed, darling; it flushes away the dirt."

And so it is with tears. Tears are good.

Yet many people feel uncomfortable when someone is weeping, alarmed at the sense of disintegration, of things going wrong, and at the sense of responsibility that comes in the company of someone so vulnerable.

I remember very vividly watching a small group of mourners arrive at an elderly woman's funeral. The husband of the deceased woman was in the centre of the group, clearly on the verge of tears. He had lost his beloved companion of over sixty years. His sister, standing close to him, was urging him not to cry: "Come along, Jack! Be a man! Keep your chin up!" It was their way – to weep in a public place would have felt deeply embarrassing to that family – but surely it should be acceptable to shed tears at the funeral of your wife?

Our tears are often held back, to be expressed in times of privacy. If we can help it, we do not weep on the railway station, in the library, in the hotel foyer. We weep in the solitude of our own room at home, in the arms of those we love and trust, in the protective space of the wide shore as we sit looking out at the ocean.

It is comforting, healing, or supportive, to people who have lost their homes and everything in them, to allow them to feel they can cry. People ought to be allowed to shed their tears when they have lost everything. There should be enough sense of privacy and there should be someone they can trust and confide in to make this possible.

Who will there be, in a care home, to sit with newcomers who need to shed tears at the loss and sadness of leaving the familiarity of home? Maybe a member of the family, who has come with the new resident to help them settle in. But some people are even more embarrassed by expression of emotion in their own family than with strangers. Maybe one of the care staff will have time to sit with the new resident, talk quietly together, allow some the emotion of what must be processed to overflow. But care staff are often pressed for time, occupied with residents' meals, helping them to the bathroom or to wash and get into bed. If the resident–staff ratio is high, it may be that the only time the care staff have to listen to residents is when they are helping them on the toilet. And although, in general, care staff are likely to be more comfortable with the expression of what is usually private – emotion, bodily functions – than the general public may be, some members of staff will be more at ease with people who are overwhelmed with sorrow than others. A chaplain or trained volunteer may have a very helpful role to play here, having both the understanding and the time to spend specifically on what is happening in a person's inner world. There may also be a key worker assigned to the new resident, who will build a particular relationship and take time to listen and to understand.

Even at such momentous times of change, there will be some making the transition to living in care accommodation who have come to terms with the tearing pain of loss. Some will have gradually downsized their possessions in a wise, strategic manner, maybe making a series of house moves from the large family home to the retirement bungalow to the warden flat and now finally to a residential care home or nursing home room. Some will have spent a long time in hospital considering what to do for the best – going through the options, making arrangements – and will have gone through a process of accepting the necessity for change. Some will be simply in shock – bewildered, not knowing how to be or who to be in these unfamiliar surroundings, with the soothing routines of home all entirely evaporated.

Some new residents may have come unwillingly to this new place and may be frightened or belligerently defensive. They will need extra reassurance as they come to terms with the changes in their lives – and, if they are noisy or disorientated and confused, it may be a time when extra support is needed for all the residents, who may find the newcomer distressing or alarming.

If the care staff, chaplains, and volunteers in our care homes, and the relatives of those who must leave their own home, have the maturity and confidence within themselves to consider and behold the emotions and responses of those who leave their independence behind – *even when they cannot fix it* – they will be agents of healing and reassurance.

To hear the stories of times now gone also helps. Even when someone has left the familiar setting of their own home for a room that presents an entirely different kind of environment, memories have vitality and power to recreate a sense of personal history and identity.

Martha was like a statue, calm and stoical and pale: it was hard to know what she thought or what she had heard, or even if her wits were entirely functioning. But one day as I sat beside her and took time to chat, I realized that in fact she was simply far away most of the time. As she talked about the dairy farm, about taking the cows for milking across the hill where a wide and busy road now hummed with traffic night and day, about primrosing in the spring along the hedgerows of Three Oaks and Westfield, she began to come alive. As she told me how her brother had helped her and Tom to buy the cottage when the chance came – but they had paid the money back, yes, every penny– and as she remembered the winter they had walked to chapel along the tops of the hedges because the snow was so deep, I saw the only animation on Martha's face I had ever seen. She needed to relive the past to live at all.

In helping people to make the transition required when they leave behind the home that was the repository of so much experience and memory, the chaplain, visitor, or care assistant who has the time to listen may offer more than they will ever know: the chance once again to touch what was held so dear.

Regret for what might have been

It is not always recognized that when we can no longer live in our own homes, we are losing not only what we had but also the chance for what we didn't have.

Perversely, the loss of what we never had can bring a far deeper grief than the loss of what we have had.

You can observe this in the lives of adult children mourning the death of a parent who did not love them. They suffer a double grief: the loss of the person who has died and the loss of hope for a breakthrough or reconciliation one day.

You can see it also in people struggling with one of the great challenges of middle age: the acceptance of mediocrity – the recognition that I will always be an assistant teacher, never a head; that I may be the star of the amateur dramatic society, but I don't have quite what it takes to go professional; that I will never make a million; that when fifty years of working life have gone by, I will have paid off the mortgage on this budget villa with its rather inadequate garden – and that will be my life's achievement.

The small half of what we lose is what we had; the greater half is the loss of the things that might have been.

This loss is exacerbated by our tendency to assume that what might have been would inevitably have been good. So, when a nun talks about choosing a celibate life in community, she may fantasize that in making this choice she gave up the chance to have a husband who loved her, a family of children, and a home of her own. I never met a nun who imagined that what she gave up was a cramped and vulnerable life of lonely singledom (never met the right person somehow), or a marriage soured by the sadness and frustration of infertility, or the terror and grind of living with a violent man who drank too much and sexually abused his children. It was never *that* sort of life the nun imagined she had given up – more the cottage with roses round the door.

Similarly, the man who is disabled by a stroke in his

forties and can no longer manage at home is unlikely to say to himself, "Actually, I would never have amounted to much anyway – I'm lucky to get my bills paid here, because I certainly never managed to cover them on the wages I could earn."

No. The loss of what might have been is *massive*, as big as our imagination; you could say it is the losing of our dreams. And although the great future may have existed only in our imagination, the loss nonetheless is very real.

Although mourning for what might have been is a human inevitability, it is not an occupation that feeds the soul. The most helpful place to start any journey of the soul will always be "what is real, now". What could be, should be, or might be true is likely to include a few water bombs of disappointment.

To honour and touch gently the real journey of the real past, to open one's hands and permit what might have been to go, to look honestly at present limitations – all these are necessary stages in coming to terms with present reality. The way in to real peace will always be through engagement with one's actual circumstances; the surest way for grief over what might have been to lose its hold, is for realistic hopes for a real future to begin to build.

Hopes for the future

Have you ever made a vision board? These are helpful envisioning tools that enable us to sharpen our focus on how we would like our life to be. It's possible to make a vision board electronically, using text boxes and cutting and pasting internet images; or you can use good old-fashioned marker pens and paper, scissors, and glue, cutting out magazine pictures and sticking them on to a fair-sized rectangle of cardboard.

The vision board includes images of the way of life you choose and desire, along with affirmations and descriptions of what you would like to achieve and see manifested in your life.

If I were considering exchanging living in my own home for residential care, on my vision board I would have, right there in the middle, a picture of a view of trees through a big, low window. If I had such a view, I would be well on the way to realizing what I need to be happy. I would also include a picture of a large plateful of healthy salad – I don't know how I would cope on a diet of white-bread sandwiches, tiny helpings of vegetables, and abundant biscuits, cake, and scones! I'd have pictures of a cat and a dog – I'd love to live somewhere where they had a resident cat and visiting pat-dogs. I would add a picture of someone in a room on her own: privacy is profoundly important to me. I might add simple affirmations such as "peace and kindness", "quietness", "respect", "people who understand me", and "no streetlights shining in through my window".

When my vision board was all finished, I would take it with me when I went to visit prospective accommodation. Often I become intimidated, inhibited, and tongue-tied in interview situations, obsessed with being pleasant and polite, and what is important to me vanishes from my mind completely. With my vision board, I would be able to start making an assessment of whether I could be happy in this place.

A vision board essentially aims high. It is a concept arising from philosophies of positive thinking which embrace the conviction that we "dream" our world – we manifest our life experience by our thoughts; what we pay attention to, we get more of. This is observably true, and it takes very little reflection to see that sharpening the focus of our hopes, dreams, and priorities, by such means as making a vision board, significantly increases the likelihood of realizing them.

Although even pessimists would surely concede this, many remain sceptical of the extent that we can really influence what happens to us by the application of conviction and focused, sustained envisioning.

It may also be helpful, therefore, to make a list of our hopes and dreams, and another one of our fears and dreads, creating two spreadsheets: one shading from "basic non-negotiable requirements" to "personal ideal"; the other shading from "worst-case scenario" through "acceptable, I suppose" to "what I would like best if I can choose".

It's hard to project forward very far with some of the things that might be included on our lists. For me, at the present time, one of my "basic non-negotiable requirements" would be to enjoy complete privacy for bowel movements. I should absolutely require a single room with an en suite bathroom. But that's *now*. It may be that a time will come when I cannot go to the bathroom without the help of a hoist or a wheelchair, or that I may enter residential care having had a colostomy bag fitted: in which case the parameters all change, and, as I learn to adapt to the new me, my priorities would correspondingly alter also.

On the other hand, there are some things I know will never change. Whatever happens to me, to feel the sunshine and the breeze, to hear the birds sing, and watch the seasons change will remain necessary food for my soul. Even if I lose my sight, to sit where I can smell the garden, feel the morning rise, and hear the first tentative notes of a blackbird in the dawn would mean the world to me. Even if I lose my hearing, to be where I can see the colours of the new day and the sunset would feed my soul. I ask myself: can I really insist on this? In a world where destitute people bear hideous cancers in the gutter, can I ask for a room with a view? So I have to decide: where on the spectrum do I place this, in real terms? Is it a "personal ideal", something I long for, but cannot insist upon? Or is it a "non-negotiable basic requirement", more important to me than cleanliness or kindness, than high-quality nutrition, adequate medication, privacy, or financial considerations?

Some people may prioritize a preference for eating in privacy. In a nursing home, it may be normal for residents to take their meals in their own rooms, but in a residential care home they may be encouraged to join the others in the dining room. Sometimes a respite client whose spouse has just died will want to be alone in their room and have meals brought to them. In some places that will be accepted; in others the view is taken that it is therapeutic for them to come to the dining room to socialize. Some residential homes place a great emphasis on socializing – with a living area where lots of clients sit and chat – whereas others do not prioritize the community aspect of residency, and clients stay mostly in their rooms. So it is important to match the care home's approach to socializing with that of the prospective resident. Thinking through our personal priorities beforehand will help us to clarify and focus, so that we choose wisely in finding a new place to call home. Undertaking such an exercise of envisioning and thinking through helps us to know ourselves, and to enter imaginatively the options and experience of those we care for or work with, who are making the transition from living in their own homes to residential care.

To talk these matters through with people whose situation requires them now to seek out accommodation in a care home will help them to bring into clarity, into itemized order, what is probably a confused and unexamined blend of preferences and dread, a felted mat of likes and dislikes that have never been systematically considered and prioritized.

It helps to nail this right down – get a list on paper, logged into a spreadsheet with a strong visual differentiation. Perhaps a page shaded like these examples:

Non-negotiable	Appreciated	Desirable	Personal ideal
MRSA-conscious staff	Visiting library	Position by a window with a view of a tree	Somewhere with a Christian ethos

Vegetables on daily menu			

or this:

Couldn't care less	Not fussed	Care passionately
Outings and socials	Chaplains visiting	Cleanliness
Visiting hairdresser	Fresh flowers on display	

or like this:

Worst-case scenario	Bullying staff			
No thanks	Untrained staff	Staff leaving radio/TV on in my room		
Could learn to cope	Shared room	Poor quality food	Unappealing common room	
Bearable	Commode instead of bathroom	Being left alone all day		
Best	Single en suite room	Fresh vegetables	Located near my family	Sunny room

However such spreadsheets are formulated, they create a concise form of record-keeping for the planning and preparation in making the transition from living independently to residential care accommodation.

They are useful in communicating with the managers of homes on the list of possible choices, because they provide at-a-glance information. People often get flustered at interviews, especially if things do not progress in the way they had imagined and mentally rehearsed; and when we are flustered, we find it hard to make use of preparatory notes when they are formulated as several pages of jottings in a notepad. Small, easy-reference, single-page spreadsheets like these are more helpful, and copies can be made so that the manager and the prospective resident can look at them together.[2]

Personal standards, expectations, and priorities

Our hopes and fears will be conditioned by our past experience, our family and cultural background, and our personal standards, expectations of life, and priorities.

Because these are an intrinsic part of who we are, how we grew up, and our personal history, they often remain at the level of unexamined assumptions – and the deeper their roots in our psyche, the more true that is likely to be.

It can be very helpful, therefore, in finding our niche in a community setting, to have a wise companion – whether a chaplain, a nurse or care assistant, a volunteer, or someone from among our own friends and family – to help us reflect upon and consciously express what is important to us, what motivates us, what opinions and beliefs determine our visceral reactions.

It is a time for honesty. If Mother holds extremely racist views, and she is going into a residential home where all the residents and care assistants are white, and hers will be the only brown face, it may be better for her to face honestly that she detests white people, and find a situation where she will feel less threatened, than to try to suppress or deny an attitude which may not be politically correct but is likely to become a source of distress.

I know that one of my own expectations of life is courtesy. If the time came for me to live in a nursing home, I could be very forgiving of clumsiness and human error, and I would not be especially fussy about schedules and timetables – if eleven o'clock found me still sitting in my dressing-gown, unwashed, because the day staff had got behind, that would not trouble me in the slightest – but if I were treated with discourtesy and contempt, the sparks would fly.

I know also that treats are very important to me. I have to have something to look forward to. Even if I am adequately housed, clothed, and fed, if there is no fun, no special occasion, no highlight to the week, my mood becomes very low very quickly. My treats are such things as a magazine once a month, a piece of cake or a chocolate in the afternoon, a good film on the television – nothing expensive or ambitious, but little things that make a real difference to my sense of well-being.

It is also very important to me to be close to my family. I lead a solitary life now, so days passing when I saw no one but a care assistant with a breakfast tray... lunch tray... supper tray... would not be a source of suffering. But to know that in the course of a week different family members would be calling by for a half-hour chat would mean the world to me.

My living standards have never been especially high. I am not house-proud. Our home is not dirty, but the shine on the floor wouldn't hurt your eyes. I vacuum the middle bits of the room tolerably often, but the spiders are safe behind the sofa. I am not meticulous about washing grapes and apples before I eat them – I do it sometimes. In our house nothing matches and most things are second-hand. So if I went into nursing care, pristine carpets, pale wood bedroom furniture matching throughout, crisp chintz curtains, and accessorized lampshades would feel distinctly alienating. I like things a little old-fashioned. I like odd-shaped attic rooms tucked in the eaves of the building and conservatories that are kind of returning to the wild.

And deeply, with a passion, I hate uniforms.

My mother, on the other hand, trained as a nurse and devoted to the decor of her homes, would find a starched blue and white uniform soothing to her soul, and elegant furnishings and five-star bathrooms essential to her personal well-being.

Our standards, priorities, and expectations are intensely personal and condition our hopes and the things of which we are afraid.

At the centre of good care provision is the personal, so the essence of a good selection process includes the ability to gain trust and establish rapport, to ask the right questions, to give people the time to reflect upon and identify what is important to them, and then formulate the results of that reflection into easily assimilated data.

Points to remember

• Although most older people dread the loss of their independence and fear making a transition into residential care, this step can bring a new lease of life and a dramatic improvement in relationships with close family members who have been acting as carers.

• Researching information about suitable residential accommodation may usefully include contacting informal local networks such as Freecycle or faith groups, in addition to the usual avenues of enquiry such as published inspection reports and organizations with a specific brief of supporting and advising older people.

• Leaving one's home for the last time is a profound and comprehensive bereavement; grief at what is lost and a space to remember and to shed tears are appropriate and helpful in making this great transition. This looking back may also include the expression of regret for what might have been and will now never be.

• Part of a constructive transition will include envisaging and developing hopes and plans for the future. Such simple envisioning tools as vision boards, charts, and spreadsheets can assist in the helpful formulation and easy communication of these hopes and plans.

• In choosing an appropriate residential setting, it is important to come to a realistic assessment of the prospective resident's standards, priorities, and expectations, as well as their clinical status and nursing requirements.

CHAPTER 2

Families and friends

At eighty-two, Angela became increasingly frail. She had several falls. She became increasingly deaf, forgetful, and suspicious. She needed her adult children very much, but found it hard to trust them. They had a lot to forgive as her attitude to them was sometimes accusatory and hostile. She felt vulnerable and afraid. She was unwilling to invite strangers into her home or allow neighbours to have a key. After she had a fall inside a locked house, followed by a spell in hospital, her son fitted a key-pad entry system to her home and arranged carers to call each day, but it became apparent that Angela really needed 24-hour supervision. Nobody knew quite what to do.

Then another hospital stay became necessary. In the hospital, disorientated, Angela believed herself to be at home. She was assessed as too vulnerable to return to living in her own home, and, with help from hospital staff, her sons found her a place in a nursing home.

She settled in well, but did not know where she was. When one of her sons visited, she would clutch his hand and beg him to take her home when it was time for him to leave. He found this deeply upsetting, and he felt ashamed that his brother seemed to cope better with the distress than he did. He found it hard to make himself visit and often stayed away, though his brother visited several times a week. He wasn't sure how much this mattered: Angela's perception of how long it had been since they visited was an expression of how much she missed them, not how much time had elapsed. They could go for a coffee and she thought a fortnight had passed.

Meanwhile, the two brothers began to tackle the immense task of bringing into good order the family house and garden. Angela had lived there with severe mobility difficulties for many years – there was everything to be done.

For these two men, their mother's transition into care was very demanding. They felt strongly their duty to her, and, loving her very much, they wanted to do all that they could. Yet her attitude to them, as senility advanced, was unpredictable and often hurtful. Their offers of help were not always appreciated. There was a great deal to accomplish. The renovation of the house; the research and establishment of first the temporary care package, then the residential place; the monitoring of that; the intensive visiting; and the problem of how and when to dispose of the house – these responsibilities were complicated, time-consuming, emotionally draining, and large scale.

Elaine

Elaine was widowed in her seventies and coped well. A reserved, private personality, she did not share or openly display her grief. She managed well alone until she developed cancer at about eighty years old. When this happened, although she was not in need of nursing, she concluded that it would be wise to move into residential care accommodation. Not a driver, she asked her son (her only child) if he would mind taking her to visit two or three care homes she had identified as possibly suiting her needs. Over two weekends he went with her, and she chose the place she liked. Elaine booked herself in, made all the arrangements, disposed of most of her personal possessions, and moved out of her house. Her son, at her request, then put her home on the market (all was neat and tidy and in very good order), had the remaining furniture and utensils removed by a house clearance firm, and that was that. He visited her regularly over the next few months, at the end of which time Elaine died. She had been well cared for, calm, and in control throughout. She needed help in certain areas, but was able to oversee and stay in control of her affairs, which meant a lot to her. Crucially, Elaine recognized, identified, and accepted what would be necessary before problems materialized. It takes courage and the ability to think objectively to achieve that, and not all people are capable of this.

Ruby

Ruby, too, lived in the home where she had raised her son (also an only child) until she reached her late eighties; by then she was a widow. The choice of a residential care home was easy in her case. She was old, but had no specific illnesses, and there was a residential care home connected with the church where her husband had been the organist for decades – an important position in a large church with a considerable musical tradition. So the move incorporated a sense of continuity and belonging; indeed, she moved from a relatively lonely and isolated situation to a context in which she had been known and belonged for many years. Unusually, in Ruby's case, her sense of identity was probably strengthened rather than diminished by leaving her home and moving into residential care.

She also was emotionally insulated against the wrench of leaving the familiar in that, unlike Elaine, she did not sort through her possessions or make any preparations at all for her move. With the help of her son, she advertised the house for sale successfully, but made no arrangements to move before the purchasers were to take possession of the house. On that day, her son came at her request to help her move. Nothing was packed, nothing finalized – the butter was still in the butter dish and her fridge full of food, while the new occupants of the house sat outside waiting to be given access.

Ruby did not find this move particularly stressful, but her son and daughter-in-law did.

In the residential care home to which she moved, the

rooms were unfurnished, allowing the residents to keep around them their own familiar possessions and making the new environment feel immediately like home.

Kate

Kate lived with her mentally ill daughter and her son-in-law (a man with a history of mental cruelty). She was blind and, being relatively immobile as a result, she became increasingly frail and subject to respiratory infections as she entered her eighties. Although it became apparent that she would benefit from residential nursing care, her son-in-law was reluctant to allow the release of monies from her estate for the large sums this benefit would incur. Therefore, although Kate was taken into hospital and was not well enough to return home, a nursing home place was not found for her. Kate had two other daughters and a son. In this very traditional family, nursing care was seen as the responsibility of women: although her son loved her and visited her in hospital, he did not perceive himself as able to contribute a solution. The daughter Kate lived with was herself too vulnerable to organize the care provision Kate needed. Of her other two daughters, one was also a fragile and indecisive personality, and the other was hampered by being the temporary sole carer for her two-year-old grandchild.

So Kate lingered on in the hospital. She was on a busy ward where the staff did not expect to provide the full range of services normal in a nursing home. Weak and ill, Kate could not look after herself well. Slightly confused away from her home, and blind, she was not able to feed herself. The nurses in the ward put her meals and drinks in front of her, then later removed them, untouched. She was not helped unless her relatives came in. She was not washed or kept tidy.

Kate's family never did find it within themselves to challenge the stance of her son-in-law, and in the end they ran out of time. Dehydrated, neglected, lost between incompetent nurses in a badly-run ward and family members unable to meet the task of arranging alternative provision, Kate died an unenviable death, alone.

Sybil

Sybil – a fit, active, intelligent widow in her seventies, interested in life and people, a happy, engaging personality – sold her home and took a room in a residential care home. She benefited from settling in while still in full control of all her faculties. She learned the route from the residential care home to her beloved church and drove there regularly. The staff came to know and love Sybil while she was still fully herself, and it was with a sense of being in her own home that she eventually and gradually made the descent into the frailty of old age.

Sybil had four children – all loving, helpful, and supportive – but apart from sustaining their personal relationships with her and visiting her regularly, her arrangements asked nothing of them at all.

41

Joyce

Joyce had six articulate and highly educated children: a close-knit family in which she was unquestionably the lynch-pin – a real matriarch. When her health began to deteriorate and a diagnosis of Alzheimer's disease was obtained, her family was thrown into disarray as they began to make the arrangements for her transition into nursing care. Without Joyce leading from the front, the family dynamics had to be entirely renegotiated. All the children were strong personalities, but different perspectives on gender roles (some were feminists, some more traditional) and, in some cases, a hierarchical understanding of birth order meant that resentments and antagonism flared among the siblings. All of them loved their mother, but all of them were fully involved in career positions of considerable responsibility. Anxiety about the adequacy of their own responses, coupled with insecurity about comparative performance in carrying out their family duties, made the arrangement of Joyce's care provision lengthy, wordy, and uneasy.

In spite of the uncomfortable emotional journey this family went through, they ensured that the very best quality of care was found for Joyce, and they visited her and put all her affairs in order most conscientiously.

Stella

Not long after the death of one of her two beloved sons in a traffic accident, while the family was still deep in grief, Stella was diagnosed with breast cancer. Married, with her surviving son still living at home, her family undertook to provide her care. In practice, this meant that Stella spent most of her time quietly coping with the aftermath of surgery, chemotherapy, and radiotherapy on her own at home, as her husband was self-employed and compassionate leave was not an option, and her son was out at work. Hospital volunteer drivers took Stella to and from her clinical appointments, and she did what she could to live normally, encouraging herself, in the daily journal she kept, to be less selfish, to focus on the needs of her husband and son, and to keep going. Stella's home was deep in the English countryside. A gardener and an artist, she loved the trees and birds, all wild creatures, and all green and growing things. Although her situation left her in solitude much of the time, this held no fears for Stella; she was content and at peace in her own cottage. Her health eventually deteriorated to the condition where it was felt appropriate for her to be admitted to the hospice in a nearby town, and so it was only in the last few weeks of her life that Stella left her cottage on the edge of the woods for the nursing care she now needed. Her husband and son visited her faithfully, she died very peacefully, and her belongings remained in the cottage just as she had left them, ever after – as though she might at any moment walk in through the door.

Observing the mothers of these families make the transition from living in their own homes to residential care accommodation, the most striking thing to me is how different from each other, how individual, they all are.

Even so, there is one reality which emerges: the happiest outcomes are likely to be reached by preparation, well in advance, and ideally by the person who will need to make the transition into residential care accommodation. Families will be more or less supportive, not necessarily because they care more or less, but according to their backgrounds, temperament, and experience. There are many things to be organized – finance and property, paperwork and research – and not everyone can envisage or manage the tasks involved. Just muddling on, though it may present difficulties increasing in a steep curve, is the line of least resistance.

In negotiating the transition from living independently, there are some hurdles to overcome, encountered not by everyone, but by many families.

Love

One of the big challenges, perhaps surprisingly, is love.

We often think of parental love – a mother's love particularly – as unconditional: a total, irrational devotion to her child. Although traditionally it is portrayed in this way, the love of a parent for a child is more complex than that. Parents often project on to their children their own aspirations and prejudices, and the child can be a conduit for dreams and hopes unfulfilled in the parents' own lives. Parents also often regard their children as a resource that will supply them with certain benefits as of right. This comes to light vividly when homosexual children "come out" to their parents – often the response is disappointment and reproach that the parents are now unlikely to be provided with grandchildren. More often than not, parents look to their children to develop in line with their own ambitions – pressuring and bribing them towards academic or sporting success, encouraging by the expression of strong approval or disapproval the adoption of the parents' preferred mode of dress and adornment. Many a tearful scene has been caused at home by a pierced lip or a prominent tattoo. Parents expect to have a say in (and often control over) how their children dress their hair, whom they choose as friends, what vocations they follow, how they raise their own children. Parental love is, in fact, far from unconditional, and in many families love is a tool for coercion, to be withdrawn as a form of punishment.

But the love of a child for their parent *is* unconditional, and sometimes remains so despite every setback and discouragement. There are some children who heartily loathe their parents, but usually with good reason. There are some children who simply cannot relate to one or other of their parents, but in that case they are usually disproportionately devoted to the other parent.

The path of any kind of love is never a smooth or easy journey, and all loves have their moments of dismay.

When a person is in need of more care than living in their own home or living with a family member can provide, and the time comes to make the transition to residential care accommodation, one of the difficulties is love.

It is because children love their parents, and because

it is seen by everyone as the responsibility of children to manage this transition for their parents, that the transition is so difficult for the children.

Angela's sons are a good example of this. The somewhat paranoid characteristic of her increasing senility hurt them deeply, in a way that it would not have done had she been someone else's mother. That she accused them of neglect and ceased to trust them was immensely painful; the more so because they could not protect themselves and allow recovery time by keeping a little distance – she needed them the next day because she'd fallen again.

When she went into hospital, they both felt a strong sense of duty to visit her, as well as putting in their best efforts to sort out her house and financial affairs. When they visited her and she clung to their hands, begging them to take her home with them (even though she was well cared for and perceived herself to be in her own home), it wrung their hearts and made them feel wretched.

These interactions with their mother touched these men at the very roots of their being: they felt inadequate, they felt mean and cruel, they felt ashamed – although, in fact, they were working round the clock to do their very best for her and make life as easy and happy for her as it was in their power to do.

If they had not loved their mother, or if she had been someone else's mother, they would have felt sorry for her, but the interactions would not have had the power to reach into their souls and touch them so deeply. The *pain* of loving results in much of the avoidance that leads to people struggling on inappropriately long after they needed to be rehoused, nursed, and looked after.

Respect

As well as the unconditional love of a child for their parent, another issue that complicates the management of the transition process is respect.

The culture and morality of a society are formed from that society's religion, and every religion makes a strong emphasis on an attitude of respect towards older people in general and one's parents in particular. Even in a secularized, post-religious society, religion will be at the foundations of traditional morality and culture, and respect for parents and elders will be in there somewhere. It is in the foundation of what we expect of ourselves: you can be sure that thugs who attack, rape, and steal from old people are individuals who suffer from profound loss of self-respect, acting outside the boundaries of their culture's moral foundation.

When a parent becomes confused and forgetful, or is no longer capable of attending to personal hygiene and keeping their home clean and tidy enough to be safe and comfortable, it is the children who are expected to step in. At this point, the whole relationship has to be renegotiated.

Most parents expect obedience and compliance from their children, as part of the culture of respect. When children are little, it is commonplace to hear parents ordering their children about: "Come along – quickly!"; "Get in that car!"; "Look at me when I'm speaking to you!"; "Wipe that grin off your face!"; "Never mind '*why?*' – you do it because I say so!"; "Get off that phone!"; "Take that skirt off and change into something decent!" Familiar?

The expectation is that with grace, or with tears and sulks, the child will comply with the orders of the parent. In most families, this goes on from day zero until the day the child leaves home. An expectation of duty continues after the child leaves home. I have often heard parents complain bitterly that their daughter does not visit, or their son does nothing to help them with the overgrown garden. I cannot recall hearing an adult child express the same *expectation* of a parent, though they may feel disappointed to experience indifference or lack of support.

Renegotiating the relationship

The difficulty arises at the crossover point: when the expectation of help and support reaches the level where the expectation of obedience and compliance can no longer be met. In order for the parent to be safe, clean, and adequately fed, their clearly stated preference to live independently can no longer be accommodated. This is devastating for both the parent and the children. Unable to carry out both the needs and wishes of the parent, the children feel that they have let their parent down and disappointed them; they are no longer good people. The parent, seeing their authority no longer able to dominate the unfolding of events, feels humiliated and outraged. This forms an unhappy mixture with the fear and sense of vulnerability engendered by failing physical strength and failing memory.

These uncomfortable emotions belong to the period of renegotiating the relationship that typically happens *before* the vulnerable individual enters care accommodation. Part of the reason it is so painful is that there is no third party to help mediate: the children and the parents are all interested parties in the emotional transactions belonging to this period of change.

Third parties

It may be helpful for the children who have to manage their parents' transition from living in their own homes to seek the help of some wise and respected friend, counsellor, or advisor – a minister, nurse, or social worker, perhaps – in talking through strategies and plans for the future. Not only is such a third party outside the web of family relationships, with all its complex emotional history adding the weight of connotations to the challenge of present difficulties, but their presence may also encourage restraint and courtesy in the discussions that cannot always be relied upon in family-only encounters.

Such an experienced friend or advisor can also be helpful in providing the information that will help determine what is and what is not realistic and available for this individual in this local area.

A series of meetings to discuss helpful ways to proceed, instigated before the situation gets desperate, is likely to achieve a better outcome than one meeting arranged at a time when the home is in disarray, the vulnerable individual is in hospital or badly confused, and anxiety is running high.

It is particularly constructive to have meetings specifically and expressly to discuss ways forward, with a third party involved: the designation of the time for the task means that the issue will not be avoided simply because, when it came to it, nobody liked to broach the subject. It's a good idea to have a series of meetings (perhaps three) rather than just one, because strong feelings modify, develop, and are subject to reconsideration; a series of meetings gives a better chance of the right outcome being mutually recognized rather than forced by one party upon another.

Emotional honesty

It is helpful in the course of these meetings for the people involved to be honest about their feelings. The positive way to do this is to use "I" language rather than "You" language, so that the parent might say, not "You just want to get rid of me because you can't be bothered to come and visit", but "I feel unwanted, as though what matters to me isn't important any more."

When feelings are owned and expressed like this, it allows them to be heard and acknowledged, and admits the possibility of reassurance and positive regard to be expressed: "I do care about you, Mum, but I can't manage my job and my kids and look after you as much as I think you need now."

It is important to recognize that intense feelings of guilt and resentment lie around these interactions like landmines that need to be defused. At the very least, those feelings should not be exacerbated. The nursing home manager I knew who told everyone who would listen that she thought it was shocking anyway to be dumping old people in homes – in *her* culture that would never happen: the old person would be cared for by their family, there were no old folks' homes, and so on – was not contributing anything useful or constructive to the situation. We were, after all, in Bexhill-on-Sea, not Kathmandu, and had to work with the cultural parameters we'd inherited.

Now – while these people still have one another to talk to – is the time to explore, honestly but gently, the issues that are a source of hurt, to search out and affirm what is positive and can be built on, to find the ways forward that will bring security, contentment, mutual trust and respect, compassion, and peace. If resentment is unexpressed and hardens into bitterness, if guilt is unexamined, if the whole thing seems awful and wretched and difficult, when the time comes that the parent leaves this world, unresolved issues compound the grief of bereavement. What could have been gentle is made ragged and raw and hard.

Family relationships

Another hurdle to overcome in negotiating this period of transition is that it can be a time when all the players' emotional histories go live. Family relationships include a power dimension: parents wield power over children; older children wield power over younger siblings; a family member may form an alliance or protectorate with one of the others; power is often managed passive-aggressively.

There is often nothing children can do about this.

As the children of the family grow, the opportunity to distance themselves from each other and their parents is sometimes the salvation of the relationship. Siblings who fought and argued incessantly living under the same roof discover each other's attractive qualities once there is a little space between them. It is possible to cope with a domineering, critical, over-inquisitive, or implacably miserable parent in small doses: once a month for a day visit, or once a week for a cup of tea. The resentment at unfairness and being misunderstood and the guilt at being unable to make these relationships work begin to die down and matter less. Individuals find their way in the world, involve themselves in projects of their own, and form new alliances, partnerships, and households.

But when the family is reunited to undertake the complicated process of moving into a nursing home an unwilling, resentful, distressed, angry, suspicious parent, clinging desperately to the illusion that they can cope, projecting on to their children the blame for the failing situation – "If you visited me more often, I wouldn't be so lonely"; "Marjorie's son always does her garden for her"; "If only I had someone to carry the heavy groceries home from the shops, I would be able to manage"; "That? It's corned beef. No, leave it alone! That's still perfectly edible!" – the whole can of worms is opened up again.

The patronizing attitude of an older brother endured throughout childhood; the sister who has a fit of the vapours every time she is asked to make a practical contribution; even the shining example of the sister who brings home-made cakes to the aged parent and weeds their garden, cooks their dinner every day, and cannot ever leave them to go on holiday (and feels this is unfair and "Why aren't you pulling your weight a bit more?") – all this feels intolerable now.

Families survive and learn from these interactions and negotiations – most people are good at heart and bring honest concern and a desire to do what they can to help – but very few families find this transition time to be easy.

The problem is that the family dynamic grew out of the rootstock of the parents' attitudes. Now, as a parent enters a level of vulnerability that means they must be cared for, their desires overridden, their decisions vetted by their children for practicality, the whole family dynamic has to be renegotiated. It is uncomfortable, and it is not willingly undertaken for the sake of personal growth, but thrust upon all concerned by the difficult and frightening process of growing old. The aged parent – especially if weary, vulnerable, confused, and subject to consistent low-grade pain, weakness, and disturbed sleep patterns that challenge us as we grow old – is unlikely to contribute much to encourage the other family members or advance the situation.

A third party – a minister, chaplain, nursing home manager, counsellor, or wise friend – can be immensely helpful in offering a listening ear, affirming and appreciating the goodwill shown by all the family members, understanding how much this big transition asks of all concerned and the impact it makes.

Information

It is also often helpful to have the benefit of informed advice.

If full and accurate advice is obtained at the outset (and if the information relating to a range of options is gathered at the beginning), the process of transition will not be protracted by misconceptions or pointless arguments about possibilities that nobody has bothered to check.

It is worth taking time for a person to get used to the idea of leaving their home, and worth exploring and discussing the implications it raises – whether practical or emotional. It is not worth spending time arguing about finance or the merits of particular nursing homes if nobody has investigated what benefits may apply, what financial packages are available, or whether the nursing homes under discussion are expecting to have vacancies within the relevant time frame.

The internet has tremendously improved our possibilities of gathering information. Although many older people now move confidently through cyberspace, many still feel out of their depth online, so here again is an area where it may be helpful to enlist the assistance of a wise and internet-savvy friend. Just a couple of hours one afternoon can return the contact details necessary to make progress with benefits enquiries and to further investigations of recommended nursing homes with good reputations and encouraging inspection reports.

Leaving the comfort zone

Another difficulty friends and family members may experience in facing the task of helping someone come to terms with leaving their home is that the challenges and losses, the vulnerability, and personal difficulties involved may push the helpers right out of their own comfort zone.

Hugh was a retired Anglican priest in his late seventies, married to Margaret. They lived in an English village in the prosperous Home Counties, offering very welcome pastoral assistance to Father Maurice, the rector of the parish. Hugh celebrated midweek eucharists and sometimes took responsibility for the daily commitment of matins and evensong, while Margaret's cheerful and confident personality contributed much in the area of pastoral visiting. They became an integral part of the village community, loved for themselves, but a little set apart by the respect owed to Hugh's ordained status.

As they entered their eighties, they continued faithfully with these retirement duties, but by their mid-eighties health problems began to manifest. Although her constitution was in general robust, Margaret needed both hips replacing and a hospital stay became necessary. Hugh, meanwhile, had begun to rely on Margaret more and more. He had become forgetful and rather remote, he could no longer drive and relied entirely on Margaret for transport, and he had begun to suffer from urinary incontinence.

When Margaret went into hospital for her operation, the church parishioners rallied round to care for Hugh, but the incontinence proved to be a serious problem. Hugh dealt with this problem by ignoring it completely and hoping it would go away. Dismayed to find their car seats and sitting-room armchairs saturated with urine, church members felt disinclined to continue offering lifts or inviting Hugh in for supper. Inhibited by social convention and by the sense that it was inappropriate to discuss bodily functions with a clergyman, nobody wanted to raise the matter with Hugh. Somebody went to the village doctor's surgery to have a quiet word with the nurse, but nothing changed. Soon the community opinion began to form that this problem was the fault and responsibility of the rector.

"Why doesn't Father Maurice deal with this?" the parishioners muttered indignantly. "He's the rector – it's his job to tackle this!"

Why didn't Father Maurice deal with it? Probably because, like many clergymen, he was an academic, inhibited, dignified man, with a rather rarefied personality, used to dealing with people in the formal contexts of liturgy, business meetings, and short pastoral home and hospital visits – a cup of tea, twenty minutes of genteel conversation, and a brief prayer. Putting two such men together and expecting one of them to broach the subject of the other's urinary incontinence is the wild end of unrealistic.

But the sense of obligation among Christian people to

care for this elderly priest morphed into a combination of guilt and resentment when the incontinence shot the obligation right outside the comfort zone, and the guilt and resentment were conveniently projected on to the rector – "This is Father Maurice's job!"

Sometimes, we are not able to rise to the occasions life imposes upon us, and when that is the case, it is all right to say so.

Not all of us have what it takes to manage our confused and irascible elderly parents who have soiled their underwear and hidden the evidence under the hearthrug. Not all of us have the personality or upbringing that allows us to feel comfortable with undressing and washing our parents. And that is all right. Somebody has to help; we may need to play a prominent part in securing that help, but the job is not necessarily ours.

Guilt, blame, resentment – these are never constructive ingredients to add into the mix; they never improve any situation at all. In order to eliminate them, it is necessary to give both others and ourselves permission to be the people we really are.

When parents are raising their children, there will be consequences to the choices they make. If the children are never on any account allowed to see their parents naked, if the parents do not cuddle their children, if the children are not treated as equals but have a relatively formal relationship with their parents, then is it reasonable to expect that they will be comfortable with wiping Daddy's bottom when they are sixty and he is eighty-five? They may not even know how to begin the conversations that must happen in order for the parent, who is evidently no longer coping, to make the transition to a context with appropriate provision of care.

I believe that the obligations of common humanity and compassion impose a duty upon us not to ignore our fellow human beings when they are struggling and getting out of their depth, but I do not believe that being somebody's child implies responsibility for the parent's well-being. If you want your child to be comfortable talking with you about difficult issues, if you want people to be able to approach you comfortably about personal matters, if you are hoping that others will involve themselves in your life at times of vulnerability, then it is down to you to do the work to make yourself approachable. Not only is it unfair to ignore this important area of self-development and responsibility, but it greatly reduces your chances of managing the big transitions gracefully or at all.

Margaret died of a post-operative pneumonia. Hugh struggled on for a while, increasingly left alone by the church community to which he belonged, everyone (but most especially Hugh) ignoring the incontinence that cause such horror and embarrassment. In the end, he applied the only solution he could think of: he committed suicide.

Social taboos and inhibitions

Talk to your children. Talk to your friends. Talk to your spouse or partner. Learn to explore the intimate and personal spiritual and physical topics that alarm us because of our social taboos and inhibitions.

A while ago a friend underwent several months of gynaecological and bladder disorders, suffering from stubborn infections that proved resistant to medication.

In the course of this, needing to explain something that had happened to her, she described an occasion when she had stepped out of the bath and – it was difficult for her to say this – she said, "Sometimes water drips out from inside of me when I get out of the bath; it's embarrassing to mention this, but sometimes it does."

Yes. When I get out of the bath or the swimming pool, water drips out of my vagina too. And we do ourselves just the hugest favour if we can get over the social taboos that inhibit us from saying so.

Now, I am not advocating that we should importune strangers in the street with unwelcome information about the functioning of our private parts, but I do think it is healthy and wise to get comfortable with talking to *someone* about our emotions, our bodies, our finances, our relationships, our fears, our illnesses. That someone may be our children, our friends, or a professional counsellor, but to be too buttoned-up is a dangerous way to live.

Philippa was a very, very private lady who had suffered from breast cancer. She lived with, and was the carer for, her ninety-year-old mother. When Philippa discovered the lump in her breast, she felt extremely frightened, but, coming from a very reserved family who never saw her naked, Philippa could not bring herself to show or mention her discovery to anyone.

Time went on and the problem progressed. Philippa became very withdrawn and sad, and her adult children wondered if she was depressed – but didn't like to mention it. Eventually, when one of her sons saw that her ankles were becoming swollen and there seemed to be something wrong with her arm, he insisted on taking her to the doctor. By the time Philippa was examined, her cancer had progressed so far that it had exposed a rib. She had been bandaging it herself, in the privacy of her bedroom with the curtains closed – too afraid even to look.

I would identify two things as especially unhelpful for families trying to find their way through the challenges of this transition time: inhibitions and expectations.

Inhibitions that make bodily functions unmentionable and make mental confusion shameful and embarrassing do not serve us well. Expectations that assume we will fill a particular role, even though it fills us with horror and feels unbearable, also do not serve us well.

The way to safeguard against these two pitfalls is to develop open and honest relationships, to allow ourselves to be seen and known – and personally to take responsibility for making ourselves accessible and approachable enough to discuss issues such as incontinence, confusion, personal relationship, fears and hopes, and increasing frailty.

Priorities

As well as the personal communication difficulties that may be encountered when a parent becomes so vulnerable that the relationship between parent and child has to change, family members may face very challenging decisions in prioritizing their commitments.

We live in a very mobile society, and it is normal, and often strongly encouraged, for children when they grow up to move away – explore the world, go and see what's over the hill. So they do. Then while Dad at one end of the country is losing his sight and no longer very steady on his legs, his daughter has a demanding and all-consuming job as an executive at the other end of the country, already stretched to breaking point by the demands of juggling professional commitments with homemaking and raising a family.

When my husband Bernard was in hospital for surgery and tests in connection with his terminal cancer, he longed to come home, but his stay extended as more problems became apparent. Then, with no warning, his doctors decided they had done all they could. I arrived on the ward to be told I could take him home tomorrow. He was overjoyed, desperate to leave. Unfortunately, the day after "tomorrow" was also my twins' twenty-first birthday. Already my children had needed to be very understanding that Bernard (not my first husband or their father) took up so much of my time and attention. I had to tell him that though of course, he could come home as soon as possible, he would have to stay where he was until the special birthday had passed. He was devastated, bitterly disappointed. But each of us, even the most vulnerable and needy, must fit in appropriately to a family – a community – as a whole; if the needs of one are allowed to tyrannize the whole community, resentments very quickly will begin to arise.

These divided loyalties and challenging matters of prioritization include a certain duty to oneself. At times, when I was the carer for my dying husband while simultaneously fulfilling a full complement of professional duties, I felt hysterical with tiredness. It was not wise.

When my mother trained as a nurse in the 1940s, her hospital matron impressed upon her, "Your first duty is to yourself, nurse." This is sound advice.

In caring for others, in facing profound emotional challenge and significant life changes, burnout is the likely consequence of ignoring one's own human need for leisure, refreshment, and regular breaks. Sometimes it is necessary to be quite insistent about this – especially as the most demanding people often do not recognize themselves as imposing a burden.

Financial arrangements

In addition to the emotional, interpersonal, and relational challenges that may be thrown up by this period of transition, there is also often a considerable amount of daunting work to be done in the area of paperwork, finance, and property.

This will vary from one individual to another, but there is often an accumulation of documents and personal possessions acquired over a lifetime left waiting to be sorted through. Older people may have accumulated not only belongings of their own, but also the effects of deceased friends and relatives whose houses they in their turn helped to clear.

If the financial arrangements with the care home will permit this, it gives the person moving into care, and their family and friends assisting with making the transition, a helpful breathing space if the house sale and disposal of personal effects can be left until some time after the move has been made. Belongings left behind lose their emotional grip and it causes less heartache when they go. It is easier to say goodbye to one's old house when the new environment has proved comfortable and become familiar enough to feel like home.

Taking time over these tasks without rushing, seeking advice at every stage before deciding, openly admitting when an aspect of the process is emotionally difficult or overwhelming, being gentle with yourself and with each other – all will help this process of transition feel like what it is: natural, positive, and welcome.

Once the transition is made, family relationships can often move into a more comfortable dynamic, as guilt eases, difficult decisions have been faced and overcome, and the vulnerable individual is safely accommodated in a place where they can receive the care appropriate for their present situation.

Points to remember
• Every family, every person, and every situation is unique. Our experiences will vary considerably, but being organized and prepared benefits us all.

- Love is sometimes one of the most painful aspects of this time of transition. It is when we are close to someone who has become vulnerable and in need of care that the interaction between us can be challenging to manage.

- Issues of authority and respect can arise when adult children have responsibility for managing a parent's transition into residential care. The whole dynamic of the relationship may have to change.

- Enlisting the help of a third party – perhaps a wise friend, a minister, or a counsellor – can be very helpful in negotiating a way through at a time when both the practicalities of daily life and the quality of the family relationships are undergoing profound change.

- Guilt, resentment, and dishonesty are toxic and non-productive. It is wise and constructive to foster open, honest exchanges, and, again, the presence of a third party can be helpful in facilitating this.

- When a parent is experiencing the increasing frailty of age, the adult children of the family, required to cooperate in planning for the future, may find themselves uncomfortably encountering family dynamics that have long been avoided. Information reduces confusion, misunderstanding, and dissension; again, a third party to advise and chair discussions can ease the way forward.

- Decisions should not be made too precipitately. All parties involved – but especially the person making the transition to residential care – should be given sufficient time to adjust and to consider adequately the various options.

• The problems we experience, as we travel towards the time of needing to make the transition into residential care, may be embarrassing and difficult to discuss – especially for reserved and inhibited people who have not made a practice of openness in the past. We are wise to take responsibility for developing open and honest relationships with those who are close to us, so that others are not inhibited from broaching sensitive subjects with us, should that become necessary.

• As family members work together with those who are becoming vulnerable to secure the support they now need, balancing existing commitments with these new responsibilities may impose strain. It is important to keep the needs of the vulnerable individual in perspective: although they deserve attention, their needs do not necessarily outweigh the needs of those who are caring for them, or of the other relationships and commitments of the carer.

• Seeking help and advice, staying honest and open, being gentle with oneself and each other, and not rushing things, all help to move this profoundly challenging process towards a positive and successful outcome in which everyone stays friends.

CHAPTER 3

Affirming people as unique individuals

It is when we really look at people, really see them, rather than making assumptions about them according to the category we have placed them in, that we respond to them as human beings and accept them with understanding.

Identity is almost synonymous with spirituality, so it is when our identity is respected that our well-being flourishes. Perhaps the most essential aspect of helping people to make the transition from living in their own homes to settling into residential care or nursing care accommodation is to take the trouble to notice the character of the individual, to respond to that with affirmation, and to help create contexts and strategies that will protect and celebrate that sense of personal identity.

Since 1986 I have owned a wonderful Time-Life *Library of Nations* book about India. My favourite part in it is a short photo-essay entitled "Daily Life of a Calcutta Clerk", detailing the everyday routine of Sukumar Chowdhary and his family. He is described as living "with his wife, two grown-up sons, his aged mother and a maidservant in a brick house which his father built in an outlying suburb of Calcutta". The pictures (by Pablo Bartholomew) show him travelling to work, at his office desk, in the market buying betel leaves to make *pan*, returning in a rickshaw from market with his son Subir after purchasing the groceries for the day, and eating with his sons and his wife as their maidservant looks on.

The maidservant is also shown cleaning the family bathroom. Sukumar's wife Bidyut is shown cooking supper, and her sons, Subir and Sudip, are shown dismantling the mosquito netting from their beds as part of their morning routine.

Near the beginning of the essay is included a picture of the whole family, captioned:

Sukumar and his wife Bidyut pose with their sons,
22-year-old Subir and 21-year-old Sudip (wearing
glasses). Both young men have high educational goals:
the elder is working for a civil engineering diploma,
the younger for a degree in commerce. They will not
marry until they have secure jobs.

And, sure enough, there they are, dignified, slightly smiling, standing straight and proud: Sukumar, with his pen in the breast pocket of his white shirt, at the front in the middle; Bidyut, in a clean pink-and-white sari, to his right and just slightly behind him; Subir and Sudip, side by side behind their parents. Behind Sukumar and Sudip, you can see the turquoise-washed exterior wall of their home, and the door frame painted in vibrant, rich, dark green. Behind Bidyut and Subir can be seen the open doorway to the cool, deeply shadowed interior.

In the more than twenty years I have owned this book, I have returned to it often to look at this photo essay. I have been inspired and encouraged to see the dignity and simplicity of this Calcutta family and their way of life. I like to look at them standing in a row, looking out at me, smiling gently, showing me from far away across the world how life should be lived.

But one day, I was looking at this lovely photograph and something caught my eye. "Wait a minute!" I looked closer. Sukumar, Bidyut, Subir, Sudip... so... who is this?

I realized that within the darkness of the doorway, standing back a little behind Subir's right shoulder (possibly reflecting her place in the authority structure of the family, like Bidyut standing a little behind her husband?), is another figure, standing in the family group. Even in the deep shadows within the doorway, you can make out not her face, but the folds of her clean white sari. A widow would wear a white sari.

Who was this mysterious figure in the doorway? I did not think it would be the family servant, because this is intended as a formal family photograph, and she does not even sit down to eat with them. I imagined it must be Sukumar's "aged mother", Mrs Chowdhary, the one member of the family who is given no name and appears in no photographs except, perhaps, this one.

I wonder what Mrs Chowdhary felt about that?

I wonder how it felt for this family – hard-working, intelligent, able people; successful by middle-class professional Calcutta standards, but living in such material simplicity by Western standards – to be told they were to feature in a book published in America, a study of India, and their home would be there for all to see in the Time-Life *Library of Nations*? My guess is that they felt immensely proud and that they may have obtained a copy of this book and kept it as a family heirloom – just as you or I would have done.

And when the long-awaited book was finally published, and a copy came to them and they opened it to admire the pictures of their home and family life, I wonder what the nameless Mrs Chowdhary senior felt about the manner of her inclusion?

I had that book for years and returned to it again and again to study this short photo essay (which fascinated me) before I even noticed a fifth person in that family photograph. You can tell that the photographer hadn't noticed either, or she would have been mentioned in the caption. She was there but not there. And yet it was her home: the brick house that her husband, now dead, had built for her and him to live in together, the place where they had raised little Sukumar with tenderness and pride, and watched him grow into a man, responsible and successful.

I can imagine being Mrs Chowdhary, searching through the book with the rest of the family, and then feeling the intense disappointment when she had been reduced to nothing but a shadow in the only picture that included her. I can even imagine that the rest of the family may have found it amusing, and she would have had to hide her disappointment and present it as a great joke.

I wonder, too, how the photographer felt, and the publisher, about this inadvertent exclusion. I don't suppose they would be callous people, indifferent to the sense of hurt and disappointment that others might feel. My guess is that they simply didn't notice Mrs Chowdhary's presence, and absence, in the photograph. She was only an old lady, incidental to the core story

I wish I had a way to reach back to the time that photograph was taken and set this right: to give Mrs Chowdhary senior a face, a presence, a position – to restore to her the place in her own life that was rightfully her own. Nobody should be allowed, by careless oversight, to be excluded from their own life.

The individual and the system

It is very important to the staff of a care home to facilitate ways for the residents to flourish as individuals, continuing to feel affirmed as people. Especially if the nursing home or residential care home is a large one, imagination is needed to help each resident feel that they are known and considered. Nobody should ever feel like a cog in a big machine, lost in an impersonal institutional system.

When I moved from my employment as chaplain at a Methodist school to take up a new ministerial appointment, the time came for me to apply for a place for my youngest child to attend the state school local to our family's new home. Her three older sisters had secured places there and were happy. There was, however, fierce competition for places in the appropriate year for my youngest daughter. We went through an appeal procedure without success, and she stayed on as a weekly boarder at the Methodist school. In the many meetings I attended as we went through this process, I was struck by a significant difference between the two schools. In the state school (it was a very good school, and those of my children who attended had a positive experience there), the emphasis in every meeting to discuss outcomes was the well-being of the *school*. In the Methodist school, the emphasis throughout was on the well-being of the *child*. Although both schools were excellent, I felt that this significant difference in emphasis made the Methodist school's approach more conducive to the flourishing of the individual. Having said that, my second daughter felt immediately at home in the state school, whereas she had loathed the experience of education in the Methodist school.

From this I draw two lessons: first, that no one system will suit every individual, so care homes with a variety of approaches will always be helpful; and, second, that it is necessary to discern, when exploring the possibility of residency, whether the emphasis will be centred more on the well-being of the individual or on the smooth running of the community as a whole. Both aspects will be present in the care provision, but there will be this difference in emphasis. Although places that emphasize efficiency and organization will often provide excellent care, I believe it to be generally true that the chances of remaining visible as a person are much greater where the well-being of the individual is valued above the well-being of the system.

When somebody goes into residential care, they are entering a system. It will not feel quite the same as being in one's own home. There will be a system for the catering; there will be a system observed by the nursing staff to ensure that the care and medication of all the residents are well and efficiently covered; there will be a system for laundry, and name-tags on clothes will be necessary and maybe on other personal belongings as well. A friend once observed to me that, in order to get anything running smoothly, "You have to have a system"; again and again I have remembered his remark and found it to be true.

In a community of people, especially one in which the residents are vulnerable, needing support in everyday life, everything would very quickly go wrong without a system.

But people can better accept the self-discipline and compromises necessary to taking their place in community when they feel individually heard and beheld.

This doesn't add to the burden of the care staff and volunteers; it is more a matter of emphasis and approach than of adding in something extra. Most people who work in residential care homes and nursing homes have a warm and genuine interest in people and enjoy getting to know the residents as individuals, taking a pride in getting the details right for them in providing their care.

If someone new joins the care staff team, they may be told that "Bill always likes a packet of crisps with his cocoa" or "Ernie always likes a big cup". It is always the individual details that staff get to know. And they will tell the new staff member about the client's personality, or if the client is feeling tearful because of some recent sadness or upset. Even though the care staff will inevitably be kept busy, they spend time helping clients with personal care, and residents will share all kinds of things during these times. The members of the care staff come to know all sorts of personal things about the clients, understanding their preferences and their outlook on life.

Residents also enjoy as much choice in their daily life as is reasonable and possible in a communal setting. The care team works to make life as interesting and enjoyable as possible, but even if they were not inclined to do so, client choice is strongly emphasized in modern care home policy.

For example, residents can expect to be asked the day before to choose from a menu of three different meals, and they also choose what drink they have for supper.

Some years ago I was intrigued and impressed by the findings of a survey into urinary incontinence among people in residential care homes for older people. The residents were (unknown to them) divided into two groups. One group was offered choices in the matter of their daily care: when an outing was proposed, they were given a choice between two possible places to visit; when everyone was given a pot plant, they were allowed to express a preference for a pink or a blue plant. The residents in other group were still taken on an outing, still given a plant, but they were never given a choice. Among the group offered the opportunity of choice, a significant improvement in urinary continence was noted. Not only is this demonstrating (if demonstration were needed) that self-expression is vital for basic health, it also means that taking the trouble to allow individuals to have a say in what happens to them will also cut down the expenditure on incontinence pads, gloves, washing, disposal bags. And it must surely be preferable for a care assistant to spend a little more time relating with a resident's thoughts and feelings and a little less mopping up their accidents.

Another initiative I heard of, from the same enlightened continence advisor who came to address us, was the introduction of a poetry group in a residential community where there was very little for people to do together. Those who joined in with the group – listening to poetry, writing poetry, getting involved in discussion – enjoyed a marked improvement in urinary continence.

Feeling loved

The care of an individual is more than physical and medical. Clinical excellence is more than measurement and calibration and the provision of the right surgical appliances. As we know from famous experiments with which every clinician is familiar, babies die when they are not touched and talked to – when they are not loved. Nothing changes when we grow up. Of course it is necessary for our medication to be double-checked. Of course it is necessary for a supra-pubic catheter to be flushed out, or blood sugars to be monitored, dentures to be scrubbed, urine bottles to be sterilized, plastic gloves to be donned in giving personal care – but it is *just as important* for residents to know, to feel, to see, that they are loved.

Back in the 1970s, in his book *Spare The Child*,[4] W. David Wills discussed the insight that every culture contains a subculture, and that the members of the subculture will always faithfully mirror the attitudes of the members of the dominant culture.

I found this concept immensely helpful when I was raising my children, because it meant that if I saw anything to criticize in the behaviour of my children, the most effective way to change things was not by rebuke or instruction, but by correcting the behaviour (hitherto undetected!) in *myself*. It worked every time without fail.

If the parents are dishonest, the children will be too. If the parents harbour attitudes of contempt towards others, so will their children. If the parents forget courtesy, the children will follow suit.

This applies in any culture – the subculture of the pupils will reflect the dominant culture of the staff in a school, for example.

In *Spare The Child*, David Wills was writing about unhelpful, dysfunctional cultures, in which the subculture becomes a frightening parody of the regime intended by the dominant culture – yet very revealing of its reality. Wills wrote about the coming of a new headmaster, Richard

Balbernie, to an approved school for delinquent boys, in Britain in 1967. The new head had been appointed to deal with a culture of violence and bullying among the boys, which had proved too tough to root out.

When the new head arrived, instead of instigating a harsh and punitive regime to combat the callous and dangerous behaviour, he set to work establishing a new culture of respect, in which all people could be heard and beheld, and in which there was room for gentleness. I was especially intrigued by a new practice Balbernie put in place in one special unit within the school. Every evening, through the cold winter season, the members of staff were to place in each boy's bed a hot water bottle.

The point of this was that it served no purpose except kindness. It demonstrated care and concern for the well-being of the boys, and could not be interpreted as having any other motive. The new head turned that school around.

What he did was harness the psychological imperative that the subculture will faithfully mirror the dominant culture. As the staff began to show thoughtful, gentle, imaginative kindness, so did the boys.

Residential care homes also have dominant cultures and subcultures; and the prevailing sense of well-being among the residents can be greatly enhanced by addressing the sense of well-being among the staff. This can be especially noticeable when working with people with learning disabilities. If the staff are out of sorts, it affects the residents negatively, and if the staff are happy and harmonious, it affects them positively. They sense the mood and are dependent on it.

Spiritual care

I worked in a large nursing home offering palliative care to dying people and long-term care for people with chronic conditions, where a visionary matron introduced a programme of spiritual care training for her care staff.

This nursing home was linked with a hospice, into which funds poured from the local community and where the highest standards were always observed. The care staff of the nursing home saw their community as a much lowlier outfit. There was less money available, fewer appliances, a less sophisticated in-service training programme – and there were fewer nurses and more care assistants. They felt very insignificant in comparison with the beautiful place next door.

When the matron began her education programme and included the spiritual care module, it was regarded with a certain amount of bewilderment and suspicion. The cultural background of many of her staff did not include attending discussion on the ways and work of the soul. "Moving and lifting?" – yes; "Insertion of catheters?" – certainly; "Preventing the spread of disease" – OK; but "The Spiritual Role of the Auxiliary Nurse?" – er…

As the programme continued and the personality of the matron made itself felt, the mood of the whole place changed. She believed in people. She valued people. She took the trouble to understand them; she gave them a chance. She thought the best of them and sought the best for them.

Her staff began to notice the effect of the way they spoke, the way they looked. They saw the value of taking time, of listening, of treating people as valued and special – because that was how she treated them.

That nursing home became a wonderful place to be. It was, in the fullest sense, redeemed.

In lifting the atmosphere of a residential care home to becoming a place where people blossom and flourish, there are no short cuts, and the starting point is valuing the staff and putting in place practices designed to make it clear that people are loved here – practices with no purpose other than to make life nicer. When I worked in a hospice, the meal trays were always made up with a tray cloth and a tiny individual vase with a nosegay of flowers. It was a *"namaste"* – a saluting of the patient's immortal soul, precious beyond worth. It didn't cost the earth, it didn't take much time; it was simply an exercise of the imagination designed to spell out to each resident the reality that "You are worth something; you are special; you are beautiful."

Being visible

Being visible is linked to expressing preferences. The phrase "making a difference" helps us to see that. If we make no difference, we often feel we might as well not be there. When we say someone "makes a difference", we mean they matter.

It is hard to see how you matter when the smooth running of the system depends on all the residents making as little difference as possible. Change, in such circumstances, is related to problems, objections, and difficulties. Nobody changes the system just to express themselves – how annoying would that be! You have to fit in. Perhaps because of this, I have known those nursing home residents who liked to express themselves viewed with alarm and suspicion.

I remember Venetia, a lovely woman with a delightful smile; kind, alert, and positive. When we as care assistants came into her room, we were greeted with warmth and welcome, as if we were guests in her home. She enquired after our families and was interested in their doings and happenings; she told us about her family, her sons and their work, their lives.

You might have thought such a resident would be a popular member of the community, but, in fact, she made the care staff uneasy and was regarded with the deepest suspicion. I was warned about her: "Don't let her manipulate you – she's a very difficult woman." I knew her until she died, and in all that time I waited for the manipulation to begin, but it never happened.

What did people object to? She liked to have her cranberry juice in a glass jug (not from the carton), mixed with water to the dilution she preferred, and with a straw because she had trouble swallowing. She liked to wear several rings, and when she was washed at bedtime, she liked to have them taken off so her hands could be washed thoroughly and have hand-cream applied. She liked to watch *Newsnight* and *Question Time* and preferred not to be disturbed for her bedtime ritual during those programmes (before or after was fine). She liked to be comfortable in bed – and since she was completely paralysed, this was not always easy to achieve; sometimes she had to ask the care staff to come back several times, always courteously, sweetly. When she was washed, she liked to have the door to her room closed, and to have her nakedness covered with a towel, for modesty, except for the part being washed.

I never knew her be rude or ill-tempered, never heard her express anger or resentment about her condition. She was totally immobile, unable even to read unless the book was carefully propped for her, incontinent, losing her ability to swallow, but I never once heard her complain. But she was "difficult" because of the glass jug, the straws, the rings, the modesty, the TV programmes, and calling us back because she was uncomfortable. Venetia paid several hundred pounds a week to live in that residential home; I don't think she asked too much. She was "manipulative" because she made a difference; she saw herself primarily as a *person*. And – possibly even more threatening – she saw us as people too; she saw us as *the same kind of thing* as herself. Venetia did not expect that two care assistants washing or hoisting her would be chatting to each other over the top of her about their weekend date: she expected to be included in the conversation.

Losing the right to self-expression, choice, and individuality is, I think, what is usually most dreaded about making the transition into residential or nursing care.

This prioritizing of the system over the people is not usually because the staff members are unkind or themselves have an impersonal approach, but arises when there are not quite enough staff to get through all the work necessary to ensure that residents receive all the support they need. For this reason, it is more likely to be a challenge for nursing home staff than for residential care home staff. In a nursing home, it can take all the energy and time of the care assistants simply to see that everyone is clean and comfortable and fed, and it is important that everyone follows the routine closely to achieve that end. In a residential care home, although the clients need support, they are relatively able, and this gives more flexibility to the situation. The simple answer – employ more care assistants – would, of course, add considerably to the cost of the care package, which already presents a considerable challenge to some prospective residents.

Even in a busy nursing home, where it is unfair to destabilize the routine for no practical purpose other than personal preference, it is possible to find ways for residents to express the individuality of their own unique personalities.

The best care assistant I ever knew was Sean. I never saw him rush, but he got through a prodigious amount of work and could often make himself available to help out if staff were rushed on one of the other floors. Gentle and unflappable, he made everyone – both residents and colleagues – feel that they mattered to him. When he came into a client's room to wash or dress them, he always smiled at them and greeted them, explained what he was going to do, and continued to chat to them quietly as he went about the care procedures. But I think what I loved best about Sean was the way he looked at people: properly, as if he was really seeing them, considering them, caring about them. Everyone loved working with him and everyone loved being looked after by him. Like all of us, he was under pressure to complete the care routines for a large number of people within a tight time frame, but he made it seem easy. He had no more time than the rest of us, but his attitude made all the difference. Sean liked people, and when he was there, they knew they were no longer invisible because when he looked at them, they knew he had really seen them.

When I worked as pastor to a congregation, I felt acutely aware of a sensitive moment in visiting members of my church when they were staying in hospital – the moment when you look along the ward with its facing rows of beds full of patients, all looking eerily similar in their pastel nightwear, and think, "Where is she?"

I soon learned to ask at the nurse station before entering the ward, identifying the position of the bed containing my church member, so that I could move confidently past the strangers, straight as an arrow to the bed of my friend, disguising from her the awkward reality that, in her nightie, at first glance she looked just like everybody else.

It was while I was part of a hospice chaplaincy team that I learned the value of shrewd choice of bedwear. I spent a substantial amount of time with one particular patient in the hospice in the last weeks of his life: a gay man with a very strong sense of identity fought for and tenaciously retained in the teeth of social prejudice, greater then than now. I never saw him (not even once, not even on the day he died) in pyjamas. He wore *clothes*. Very weak, very thin, dependent on care staff to wash him and help him to the bathroom, confused and tired, nonetheless he was clear in his option to remain, at all times and in all circumstances, a person, not a patient. In the warmth of the hospice rooms, he chose often to wear T-shirts and boxer shorts, as he might have done sitting out in the garden on a sunny day, but it was distinctly daywear.

This, I noticed, changed the way those who approached him behaved towards him. Our clothes are probably one of our strongest ways of allowing strangers to read our personalities and form an understanding of who this is in front of them. How we dress enables people to categorize us, fit us into their frame of reference, and feel they have met us.

Personal choices

Making a clear option for personal choice encourages others to respond to us not as units but as people, enhancing the sense of each encounter between patients and staff as being a meeting of people's souls, not a category interface.

Three small, vivid experiences about personal choice have imprinted themselves unforgettably on my memory. The first was an experience recounted by a fellow student when

I was an undergraduate in my early twenties. My friend had taken a summer holiday job as a hospital porter, and he was about his work on the ward one day when he overheard a conversation between an old, sick man and a nurse. The old man, who was in the last stage of his terminal illness, was asking for a banana; the nurse was explaining that he couldn't have it because it contravened the requirements of his diet sheet. The next time my friend's portering duties took him back to that ward, the old man was dead. He never got his banana. The nurse was right, of course – it would jeopardize her job and risk the health of patients to administer unsuitable foods. That's why people dread going into institutions. If you're dying tomorrow, the banana is more important than the rules; people know that, but institutions don't. I took a funeral one time when the niece of the deceased spoke affectionately and imaginatively about her aunt. She recalled her many visits to her aunt's home and how on arrival the aunt would always have a cup of tea and a ginger biscuit ready for her. The niece sketched for us the picture of the moment when, on her own death, she came to the pearly gates: there would be her aunt waiting for her, with a ginger biscuit and a cup of tea at the ready. Listening to her made a difference to how I have lived my life, because, in focusing on the story, I realized that although it was attractive and delightful, it wasn't true. Whatever may happen to us when we die, of one thing we can be sure: there will be no more ginger biscuits and no more cups of tea. If you want them, have them now – life is fleet of foot, and it is passing, and however magnificent heaven and eternity may be, there are some things that belong only to this earth, this life, this humanity. Bananas come into that category.

The second of those vivid memories of significant details came from a terrifying and protracted relationship with a mentally unstable woman. She had young children at the same time as I did, and she was very violent towards them because of the extremity of her condition. Frightened to be alone with her, dreading her company, I was hardly able to see her as just another woman like me, until the day when she mentioned in conversation that she had chosen her house because it had a sea view, and the thing that mattered to her above all else was that she should be able to see the ocean that she loved from her home. Disconcerted, I reflected on what it meant to be so ill that you could punch and bite your toddler, lifting him up by his hair and beating him, but still really treasure and draw inspiration from your view of the sea from a bedroom window. It made me realize that every single one of us is a person, an individual; there is nobody who merely represents a category.

In the childhood room I shared with my sister, my bed was alongside the window. The white candlewick curtains had a pink lining, and outside in the garden grew a tall Scots pine where collared doves roosted among the branches. At sunrise, the room would fill gradually with pink light, and I would wake to the contented cooing of the doves. Reaching up to pull back the curtain, I would lie in bed and gaze at the birds sitting in the tree. I was entirely happy.

My bed in the house where I live today is also alongside

the window, and when I wake in the morning I pull back the curtain to look out at a tall, graceful, golden conifer, flanked by deciduous trees. I watch as flocks of birds make their way across pale grey cloud, as the sun rises in pink and gold, as white drifts of cloud like pulled cotton wool float against an azure heaven. And I am entirely happy.

It has occurred to me that, having lived a very simple life, with not much to miss in the way of status, achievement, wealth, or possessions, though I should miss strength and independence very much, I could probably still find my way to contentment if you left me in a bed alongside a window where I could see the birds and the trees and the sky. If, on the other hand, you wheeled my bed into the midst of jolly human society, under fluorescent lights, with no tranquillity, no solitude, no peace, the windows giving on to the car park or the dustbin yard, my daily prayer would be for God to take me home.

My third memory of vivid detail concerned the last days of my granny, my father's mother. Lying in her hospital bed, this stout, vigorous woman had now grown frail and very old. A member of the staff came to ask what she would choose for her tea. From among the options offered, she chose to have a boiled egg (a favourite teatime food for her). And she said, if it were possible, that she would prefer it to be soft-boiled. Again I was arrested by the consideration that, even in the momentous time of saying goodbye to this world and all it has meant to you, it still matters whether your egg is soft- or hard-boiled – possibly more so even than before. Something else about this that intrigued me is the effect it had on my mother, who was there when the conversation took place. My mother loathed this old lady with a passion – though she dutifully visited her in hospital and did what she could to take care of her – but when she heard this request, for a soft-boiled egg, she saw her mother-in-law differently – less of an archetype, more of a person – and thought more kindly of her. It was a window into the older woman's point of view – almost a first realization that she even *had* a point of view and was not merely sent here to try the patience of her relatives. Could this mean, then, that to give infirm residents in nursing homes more choice, more opportunity to express themselves, might not render them more of a nuisance but less so? Not because they would be easier to look after, but because we would identify with them better as human beings and care about them more – even the ones we found obnoxious and difficult.

Forming a strategy

Because being recognized and understood as unique individuals contributes significantly to our well-being, it seems sensible to consider ways in which we can communicate something of our history and personality when we are newcomers settling into a communal setting.

When the arrangements are made for someone to make the move into a residential care home or nursing home, there will be many questions asked in advance of the actual move, to make sure that this is the right place for this particular person and to ensure that the right care can be provided.

The care needs of the new resident will have to be discussed: mobility, personal hygiene, ability to dress themselves, level of continence, whether the client is diabetic or has any other special needs. Such information will, of course, be even more detailed when the person requires nursing care as well as a residential place.

This detailed information will be discussed in advance of moving in. At this time it will also be possible to discuss what items the new resident can bring to make their room feel like home. This will vary considerably: my own experience has ranged from a nursing home setting where rooms were shared and there was space available only for a few personal possessions – photos and ornaments, perhaps, to be displayed on a chest of drawers – to a residential care setting where the rooms were unfurnished, allowing the clients to fit their rooms entirely with familiar and beloved items brought with them from their own homes.

When the day arrives for the new resident actually to move in, the manager on duty chats to them (and to any family members who have come too) and tries to get to know them a little, and then will usually send one of the care assistants to label the clothes. This is a time of chatting to the family and the client, getting to know them and helping them feel comfortable.

Of course, everything will feel unfamiliar at first, but gradually the resident and the care staff will come to know each other as individuals.

As time goes on, there may be a visit from a volunteer or a chaplaincy team member designated to that particular new resident to ensure that they are seen as a person; loveable, vivid, unique.

It should also be said that kindness and respect ought to characterize the attitude of the resident to the care staff, as well as of the care team to the resident. Rudeness and demanding behaviour in residents is not unknown, and although care staff will understand that people who suffer from confusion or dementia, or who are simply vulnerable and fearful, may behave badly, a culture of mutual courtesy and respect is always to be encouraged.

The role of family and friends

Family members clearly have a very important role to play in helping someone make the transition from living alone to residential care. Not only will they know this individual well, but they are likely to have many similar preferences and priorities, because these are very often common to all the family members. At the time of admission to residential care, the prospective resident may be too confused, unwell, or overwhelmed to state (or even identify) the things that matter on a daily basis. If the individual is an older person (and it is most likely they will be), their daily habits will not be newly forged, so it may even be difficult for them to recognize that they are exercising preferences and priorities in the first place – living alone, those things seem just like "how life is".

I became very aware of this when I married at the end of my forties. When we went to the garden centre to buy containers for pot-plants, of course I wanted the nice old-fashioned terracotta ones, ignoring, as if they were not there, the vile, garish, bright-blue glazed pots. How disconcerted I felt when my beloved bypassed completely those dull, ugly, terracotta pots, making a beeline for the beautiful, elegant ones over there – the ones with the lovely blue glaze!

It was the same with tea and coffee. "What's this?" I wondered in horror, gazing down at the tarry liquid filling the horrid little white chimney shaped mugs. It was my beloved, making me a delicious cup of tea, passing over those ill-matched, second-hand teacups in favour of a smarter vessel, to make it extra nice.

Same when we went shopping. "Could you pick up a cake to take over to my mother's?" I would ask, never expecting him to return with a packet of some loathsome pastry and mincemeat concoctions, or something shiny and infested with figs, when what I'd imagined was a lemon drizzle cake or a fresh-cream fatless sponge.

And I just sat open-mouthed with horror when, having scraped the low-fat spread on to my toast, topping it with a translucent film of marmalade, he could have done with a plasterer's trowel for his butter and poured the jam straight from the jar! I thought the bread was the main part; he regarded it as the support act for the jam and the butter.

What makes life comfortable, cheerful, enjoyable, especially as our opportunities and possibilities become restricted by growing old or ill, is the seamless tissue of everyday preferences. Do we like the bedclothes pulled right up to our chins, or does that make us feel we can't breathe?

Do we love to have the window open, or are draughts uncomfortably painful? Do we like our cereal soggy with hot milk, or do we find it almost too disgusting to eat if the milk isn't cold and the cereal flakes still crispy? Does bright light hurt our eyes unbearably, or is "contentment" synonymous with "sunshine"?

These are the things our family members will know, but may not have the imagination to think of. A good induction process for a prospective resident would include time spent considering and discussing such preferences – with prompts and examples such as I have outlined here. Just asking "What does your father like?" is insufficient.

Even when these preferences have been communicated, it may not be easy for them immediately to become part of the pattern of daily care. Care staff often take a pride and pleasure in knowing the residents well and ensuring that they have what they need to be happy – especially when the residents are courteous and pleasant – but it takes a while to get to know the ways and idiosyncrasies of someone new. An induction process that includes creating a folder that care staff and nursing staff can refer to would encourage the process of becoming familiar with the preferences of this individual, and encourage the practice of respecting those preferences where possible.

In the early days of settling in, family members could do much good by keeping a benign eye on the progress of establishment, affirming appreciation and positive attitude, offering reassurance and a sense of continuity. It is important that the transition into residential care should be seen as marking not the cessation of family responsibility, but a new expression of it.

Family members may also be crucial in helping to select the right possessions to bring into this new context, to make it feel more like home. My friend Margery was a stained-glass artist and banner-maker, and a devout Christian believer. Her sense of identity was founded upon being an artist, a Christian, a mother, a teacher, and wife to her deceased husband. When she made the transition into care in the last year or so of her life, her son helped her to choose a stained glass panel and a banner from her collection of pieces she had made, to bring with her. These were hung ready in the room for her arrival, along with a number of other treasured possessions. Although the relinquishment of home and possessions caused her much distress, and although she was almost blind, it meant a great deal to her to have these statements of who she was and what her life had been so prominently displayed in her room.

A chaplaincy member could be very helpfully included in preparatory planning and discussions, prompting the direction of thinking with questions that need to be asked, and helping to explore the emotions that may be restless below the surface.

Friends and chaplaincy volunteers can also provide tremendous support. This is the fulcrum effect: a small action that creates a big result – just a ten-minute visit, perhaps to drop in a magazine or small posy of flowers or a beautiful piece of fruit, bringing a sense of contact with the outside world.

Handling the sense of loss

The intense bereavement of leaving one's home for the last time cannot be overstated. The sense of losing oneself in a descent into frailty is likely to be most deeply felt. To acknowledge this, without glossing over it, belittling, or denying it, is helpful.

Even so, the sense of personhood, the feeling that one still matters, will be enhanced and supported if individual preferences and priorities are given consideration in this way.

It is also not a false or empty consolation, but absolutely true, that even when much is lost, disabled, and fragmented, each of us retains our individual character and spirit: we are who we are to the end. Especially in situations where dementia clouds the picture, where words and behaviours take startling and unexpected turns, chaplains and care staff have an important role in helping family members see that this is so. Family members in their turn provide essential links and information in helping care staff to build up an accurate understanding of each new resident's background and personality.

Another important ingredient in the mixture of successfully making this big transition is humour. Not all clients are miserable, frightened, and grief-stricken; many accept this change in their circumstances with remarkable equanimity, and there are many clients who just love to have a laugh. They love banter and enjoy sharing a joke with the people who take care of them. Some people may even feel their dignity enhanced when someone makes a joke of a difficult circumstance rather than take it too seriously.

It is important to tread carefully here: nobody should be made the butt of humiliating mockery or have their problems and struggles belittled. Each person should be treated with consideration and respect. But relief from tension can be found in making light of a spilled drink, an incontinence accident, or many other trying and otherwise depressing daily challenges.

Points to remember

- Formation of a team of people to include family members, a chaplain, and a member of the staff with key-worker status in relation to the prospective resident is helpful in planning a move.

- Preparatory discussion and planning, resulting in the creation of a file for the new resident, giving details of personal preferences in everyday life – not to destabilize the daily routine of the care home or tyrannize the staff, but in order to create an opportunity to welcome the new resident as an individual – may help them feel at home.

- Input from the chaplain and a member of the care staff can help identify the right questions to ensure adequate carry-over into the care context of a sense of empowerment – the right to choose and express preferences, even when much freedom has been lost to frailty and illness.

- Guidance from the chaplain and care staff member on

the balance between personal freedom and fitting in with the community can help to clarify some crucial questions: What can realistically be offered and expected for this person in this place? Is it, therefore, the right place for this person? Will this be the right person for the community at this time?

• Imaginative selection of belongings to bring into the new context will make a big difference. What will speak to those entering the room of this resident's life and personality? Photographs from earlier years? Mementoes of past achievements? A favourite chair or picture? Clothes that will be practical for this situation but still expressive of the resident's personality and background?

• Humour, courtesy, and respect are vital ingredients in developing positive relationships as the resident acclimatizes to this new setting.

CHAPTER 4

The people and the place

When it becomes too difficult to manage at home, and someone begins to contemplate a move into a place where they will be cared for and their meals provided, I wonder what they are hoping for. Priorities will vary according to the individual, but will mainly focus on four areas:

1. Location
This is likely to be a primary consideration. People want to be near their family and friends, their faith community maybe, and in the area that is familiar to them. Even if they do not expect to be able to get out much, if at all, they still want to be where it is easy for family and friends to visit. They are more likely to know already the nursing homes in their own area, and may find it easier to imagine themselves more readily in one place than another.

2. Special ideologies and needs

This is less likely to be a primary consideration for most people, but it will be overridingly important where it is relevant. Vegans, vegetarians, Quakers, Catholics, and Evangelical Christians are among those who may prioritize the ideological foundation of a care home above the accessibility of its location or any other factor. People who have been blind or profoundly deaf for all or much of their lives are among those who might seek out accommodation specially adapted for people with a similar needs profile.

3. The staff

One of the determining factors in choosing a care home will surely be the approach and attitude of the staff. The more vulnerable a person becomes, the more important it is that staff have been selected for the attitudes of kindness, courtesy, patience, common sense, and respect that they bring with them; and then trained to a high level of competence so that they can move and lift without danger to themselves or residents, understand how to minimize the risk of spreading infection, know how to carry out all care procedures that will be required, and understand how to (and when not to) administer feeds and drinks appropriately for the well-being of their residents. A nursing home where staff have a holistic approach to care and have received training in supporting the well-being of the whole person is likely to offer a happier experience of daily living for a vulnerable person.

4. Environment

This can affect choice in a number of ways. For some people, elegance of decor is an important matter; for others, who loved the garden they are leaving, the grounds will be of significant interest. Others will be principally concerned about privacy (single rooms, en suite bathrooms, and nooks available for private conversations). Many people are drawn to places that are full of light and airy, and look to see if there is a conservatory where they can sit in the sunshine; some enjoy the traditional atmosphere of heavier, grander, more formal items of furniture and large flower arrangements. Some people love to see a place full of flowers; others are made nervous by this, believing that the flowers have all come from funerals.

Nursing homes are restricted in what they can offer to make a place feel like home by health and safety and other regulations and requirements imposed upon them, but within those restrictions they can, and usually will, respond imaginatively to the personality and preferences of their residents, to ensure that their new accommodation allows them to blossom as the people they really are.

Imaginative care takes account of personality

Violet was like a fairy: tiny, magical.

I met her while I was pastor of a church by the sea. She was on my list of old people, and a visit seemed in order. How could I have known whom I was about to encounter?

She had been referred on to our pastoral list during the time of a previous minister, by Norma who attended another church down the hill from Violet's home. Norma's church was right down near the seashore, in among the jumble of second-hand shops, greengrocers, places you could buy a shopping trolley and get your keys cut, charity shops, emporia selling Halal food and fine jewellery and reconditioned washing machines, restaurants in every flavour – Indian, Chinese, Nepalese, Thai, Greek. Opposite the end of the road to the station, by the busy crossing, just up from the bus-stop, under the great wooden crucifix bespattered with seagulls' mess that hung high on the wall of the church, Norma found Violet sunk down on her shopping trolley, too exhausted to climb the steep hill back up from the sea.

She bundled her into her car and gave her a ride home, and took her under her wing from that day, becoming a pastoral friend, getting in her groceries, and seeing to it that Violet got attached to our list, since "Methodist" was her stated church affiliation.

So I went to visit Violet, and I am unlikely to forget her.

Violet was in her late eighties, I think, at that time – so her birthdate was around the 1910 vintage. She came from a poor family who had neither the ability nor the aspiration to continue supporting her once she reached the age of sixteen. Violet did not get on well with her father.

At sixteen years old, she found herself adrift in the world, and she wanted, but could not pay for, an education. So she found work in Oxford, making her nest under the eaves of great learning, and set about studying all that she could. By day she worked hard as a maid, a cleaner; in the evening she attended every free lecture she could find, and became enriched by an extraordinary and eclectic education from some of the finest academic intellects in the country. She lived in a trailer home.

In financial terms, she stayed poor all her life, but this was hardly a hindrance. At some point she made her way to the south coast of England and settled in the basement flat where I found her when I went to introduce myself as "the new minister".

I made my way down the iron steps with care. Every one supported containers of plants. The area at the bottom of the steps was also in bloom. Margarine tubs, mushroom boxes, jam jars, old saucepans – every imaginable container had been pressed into service to accommodate Violet's garden. Daffodils and bluebells, hyacinths and crocuses, auriculas and primroses; later, forget-me-nots and valerian, lavender, anemones, nasturtiums, pansies, and wallflowers. There was even a young cherry tree making good headway in a handle-less bucket.

I tapped at the door. Although on our list, Violet had not received a pastoral visit for some time, so I had no idea what kind of a person would answer my knock. I fell in love with her at first sight. Frail, bent, probably not even five feet tall, her eyes bright with interest and her snow-white hair in a disorderly cloud of strands and random wisps, dressed from head to toe in assorted shades of lilac, she welcomed me in.

I was introduced to the cats who shared her home. In the main, they lived in the back room and Violet in the front. I am not sure that she recognized any difference in status between the human and feline species. I believe they may have been more flatmates than pets.

Somewhere in Oxford in the twenties, thirties and forties, I think Violet must have come across Rudolph Steiner and probably the Theosophists and Rosicrucians. Somewhere among the free lectures she had attended, somebody had alerted her to the principles of colour therapy, and Violet had recognized a truth in the assertion that the different colours, with their different vibrations, each contribute something uniquely edifying to the well-being of our souls.

So she painted all her furniture pea-green – wardrobe, chest of drawers, cat basket – all of it. Each day of the week she allocated to a different colour: green, blue, lilac, pink, orange, yellow, and white which held all the colours within it. Over the years she had put together an assortment of clothes, shawls, and scraps of cloth that enabled her to dress entirely in the colour of the day.

With her possessions stowed around the front room of her flat that looked out on to the riot of flowers in the basement area, Violet lived frugally and happily. Her cupboard contained (like the store cupboards of so many old people) tins of peas, cartons of dried milk, cans of vegetable soup,

Oxo cubes, Rich Tea biscuits, corned beef, and margarine. I don't recall that she had a fridge.

Violet's pride and joy was her collection of bone china tea-things. Exquisite cups and saucers (in not every case from the same set, but a near enough match) in the same colours as her clothes, and tea plates in the same clear, bright pastel shades. Some flowered, some in simple, plain, joyous colours, Violet's china celebrated the rainbow.

There were no harsh or strong colours – all were delicate, the colours of the spring. I really felt I'd met a fairy.

On several occasions I visited Violet, and we became firm friends. We discussed the philosophies of life she had encountered at Oxford, and drank tea together from cups of Royal Doulton, Minton, or Coalport, as we sat by Violet's two-bar electric fire and set the world to rights.

Nobody could say that Violet asked for much in this life. The cats who were her friends, the colours that fed her soul, the security of her own place, the flowering plants that were her joy and delight, and the several-times-a-day ritual of boiling the kettle to make a pot of tea enjoyed by the fire from a beautiful bone-china cup: and she was happy.

As time went on, I heard that Violet was to move into a residential care home. She had been unwell and was finding it hard to cope once she turned ninety. Norma had found her a place where she could live down in the basement, just as she had in her flat. The room opened on to an unused yard, so Violet's flowers were to go with her. The cats, most of the pea-green furniture, and all but a few favourites from her china collection, she had to leave behind.

I visited Violet in her new place. It was clean and comfortable; not dark and poky like the old flat. Violet sat there in a chair amid the orderly remnants of her possessions. While I was there, a member of staff brought tea on the trolley, with a cup for me as well as for Violet.

Health and safety regulations would not allow Violet an electric fire with its cosy red glow – she didn't need it, of course: no need to sit by a fire when central heating is provided throughout. Health and safety rules also could not permit Violet to make herself a cup of tea, in case she had an accident and was scalded. So her china tea things sat neatly in a glass display cupboard, where she could look at them, but not take the risk of using them. Appreciative, comfortable, but somewhat lost, Violet sat quietly alone in her fire-retardant, water-proofed chair, still marking the passing days with their allotted colours of lilac, yellow, green, pink, and blue.

Although it was not possible for her indoor routine to continue, the care home was able to affirm Violet's delight in her garden. When the move happened, to welcome her into her new accommodation, I took along a huge terracotta urn for the cherry tree. After a week or two, an agitated Violet asked me to take it away: it was too big, too grand – not her style. The cherry tree sank back into its battered old bucket with a sigh of relief.

The staff in her new home were restricted by health and safety regulations, so that Violet could no longer make her tea and sit by her fire, but it made the world of difference to her quality of life that she could continue to potter among her cherished plants. This affirmation of her choices and priorities helped her to settle in well and to accept the limitations that government regulations had imposed on staff and residents alike.

Even good care cannot solve every problem

Of course, not all people who make the transition into residential care are very old, as Violet was.

I remember Marilyn, a woman in her fifties who had struggled with MS for many years, eventually reaching a point where her family could no longer care for her at home. For Marilyn, going into care meant saying goodbye to her family, leaving behind her husband and the home they had made together. He came to visit her sometimes, and on the wall Marilyn had a photograph that showed her sitting with him and their children in a family group, but it must have felt all wrong. A husband and wife relationship is not a thing of visits and cups of tea; it is the seamless web of everyday intimacy, bedded in the context of the couple's own home, even if that is a bedsit or a trailer home or a rented studio flat. The essence of the husband and wife relationship is (for most people) that you live together.

Marilyn was not a wealthy woman, and her nursing home room was not large. A long rectangle, one end was occupied entirely by the door through which everyone came and went and the adjacent special clinical bed with its chrome bars. The other end was mostly filled with the electric recliner chair, a wheelchair draped with towels and bits and bobs, and a commode. Looking around and "reading" the room, it was possible to learn very little about Marilyn and a great deal about her condition. There was just that one picture, showing Marilyn and her family, that stated mutely, "This is where I'd rather be."

Everything had to be done for her; she could not move at all, not turn herself over or sit up in the bed – almost nothing. She could get a feeder cup to her lips and manage the bowl of food with the aid of specially modified cutlery.

In the bustle of morning feeds and washes, care assistants entered and left her room. Staff did not knock and did not always greet her. If Marilyn was being washed, someone might pop their head round the door to see if help was needed, but the enquiry was addressed not to Marilyn but to the care assistant in with her. Sometimes staff members came in just to give or seek information. When this happened, Marilyn was not always included in the conversation. She was not a very popular woman, so bonds of affection had not developed between her and the care staff, and although they were not intentionally unkind, when they were busy with their errands they did not always think to acknowledge and affirm her.

The reason she was not popular was her habit of complaining to care assistants about their colleagues. She tried by this means to set up little conspiracies and alliances, but although these did occur among the staff, nobody wanted to make them with patients. Looking back, I think these unsuccessful attempts to gain attention were probably an indication of great loneliness.

Marilyn was a tall, heavy woman, whose immobility had caused her to gain weight, and her care routine at the beginning and end of the day was time-consuming. It was with relief that her carers left her room when she was "done", but even had anyone been disposed to stay and chat, or a volunteer had come round, it was physically difficult to get close to her. The bed's position adjacent to the door made it impossible to have a bedside chair. The bed was raised high to make personal care and feeding easy. Her chair, draped with clothes and blankets, was at the other end of the room, and anyone sitting there would have been far away and lower down. Everything about Marilyn's life made her alone, and there was nothing she could do about it: she was in the best nursing home in town.

She was a pleasant and gentle person, friendly and welcoming in her demeanour, and undemanding, but the atmosphere about her was of deep unhappiness, bitterness, and misery. I could feel it, but I never heard it expressed.

Looking back, I wonder what we could have done differently. In that nursing home she would have been offered visits from the chaplaincy team and from the complementary therapists who came to give hand or foot massages to the residents who would benefit from such extra support, so there were opportunities for healing contact and conversation. But there was something we could never really reach. Perhaps Marilyn would have benefited from a regular time with a counsellor, to help her process the comprehensive – almost total – losses that illness had brought about. And perhaps there is a place for recognizing that, although we can support people and travel with them faithfully, even so we cannot fix everything.

Relationship and personal encounter

Dignity, privacy, respect, affirmation, understanding, and affection are gifts we offer each other. They cannot be demanded, and they do not occur as a result of regulations or mission statements: they appear interpersonally, new on every encounter.

Although care staff must have a tolerant and understanding attitude towards all the residents, inevitably there will be easier rapport between some individuals than others. I have not experienced this manifesting as unfairness or preferential treatment, but care assistants often appreciate the chance to care for those residents with whom a special bond has developed, and this seems to me to be natural and life-enhancing.

In residential care homes, there are usually two possible environments in which to meet the people who live there: in their own rooms or in the common areas.

Neither of these scenarios is necessarily ideal for pastoral encounter. Nursing home rooms can quickly be filled up with the equipment and commodities needed for the residents' care, and many of us would feel uncomfortable asking a visitor to sit alongside our flannels and denture powder and incontinence pads, perched on the commode. Equally, conversation can feel constrained in the communal sitting room, where others can obviously hear and see all the interaction. There would be few who felt relaxed about sharing personal matters or a time of informal prayer, observed by a number of onlookers.

In some care facilities, small group spaces are imaginatively contrived for just this purpose. A conservatory, a cul-de-sac area in an odd-shaped room, a spacious hall or landing, or the part of a room that goes into a bay window might offer the opportunity for a small group of two or three chairs and a coffee table – a place for separate, private encounter. Even where there is no separate room available, grouping the furniture to afford visual privacy can be very helpful.

Such spaces offer the chance for encounter without the sense of social inappropriateness arising from inviting someone into the bedroom when they would normally be received in the sitting room at home, and without the embarrassment of having personal conversations observed and overheard. Not only does this enhance the possibility of an enjoyable chat, it also allows new residents, coming to terms with the change from living in their own homes to living in a care home, to share their concerns and explore their emotions in an environment of relative privacy.

Remember the human

Who really knows you? How did they come to know you so well?

My children know me the best of anyone, I think. We have shared so much and faced so much together. Our commitment to each other was absolutely unquestioned.

My firstborn remarked once to her partner that she knew without a shadow of doubt that her sisters and her mother would always be there for her; she could rely on them completely. There comes a moment in the film *Gladiator* when the hero, Maximus, says to his terrified and beleaguered companions in the arena, "Whatever comes out of these gates, we've got a better chance of survival if we work together. Do you understand? If we stay together, we survive." There have been times when those words would have expressed perfectly the mindset that conjoined my children and me as we shot the rapids of the problems life delivered.

So they know me because we went through so much together, because we knew we could trust one another, because we talked about everything, because we faced and beheld so much.

My first husband knows me as well as anyone: he knows what I think and how I think. We were nineteen and twenty years of age when we became a couple, and we travelled together for twenty-five years. He has seen me at my lowest ebb. We grew up together; we made our mistakes together. The man I am married to now has had less time to get to know me; but his love and sensitivity quickly create trust and understanding.

Sometimes I make a new friend; an inexplicable chemistry draws us into a rapport. There are those people met at a party, at church, in the workplace, at the school gates; your eyes meet and you think, "Yes. I know you."

Who doesn't really know you?

Those who know me least are those with whom I have a formal or professional relationship: congregations I have pastored, colleagues, my doctor, acquaintances from any context. Those relationships are one-faceted, two-dimensional. They are also shaped by inequality. In a clinical setting, the doctor has power and superiority. In a pastoral situation, ministers have considerable status. Colleagues are often competitive in the way they relate to one another. Acquaintances are usually eager to make a good impression. Power, superiority, status, competition, and the cultivation of image have one thing in common: they do not create or encourage trust. You will never really know someone who does not trust you.

Trust is essential to well-being. If you do not trust the place and situation you are in and the people you are with, you will not be understood or contented there.

When someone makes the transition from own-home living to residential care, it is important to establish a sense that this is an environment that you can trust, where you will feel at home. Who are you? What can I expect from you? Am I safe with you? These are the unspoken questions flowing in both directions as prospective residents and their relatives meet with the manager of the home, and each begins to feel the measure of the other.

As time goes on, and the new resident settles in and becomes part of the care family, their personality and idiosyncrasies will come to be very well known indeed by the care staff. Even so, people still continue to surprise us.

In one nursing home where I worked, the care assistants

warned me about the erratic behaviour of Alice, one of the elderly residents. Alice, I was told, had become even more confused of late, carting bags of her clothes about the place. If I found her doing this, I was to return Alice and the clothes to their rightful places in her room.

Sure enough, one evening after I had been tidying away the tea things, down the stairs came Alice carrying two plastic bags full of clothes.

"What are you doing, Alice?" I asked her, in tones of pleasant enquiry.

"I'm bringing these down for the jumble sale," she said.

"What things have you got there?" I asked, and sat down with her to have a look through the bags. The contents included a golden brown, lightweight acrylic sweater in perfect condition.

"Why are you throwing this away, Alice?" I asked.

"Because I loathe the colour," she replied.

Alice was not as confused (or not about her sweaters anyway) as we thought! She just hadn't seen the need to explain herself.

Trust and boundaries

It is no mere coincidence that residents in nursing homes and residential care may especially confide in their carers when they are being washed or fed or helped on the toilet. Apart from the obvious reason that this is when the carer is devoting time to being with them, there is also something about the intimacy of the giving and receiving of personal care that promotes trust and opens the possibility of real sharing.

Care assistants often regard their work as emphatically physical, yet the intimate and personal nature of it takes them close to the residents' areas of vulnerability and implies a significant spiritual care dimension to the work.

Cheerfulness, gentleness, and respect should characterize the care relationship, and a kindly sense of humour has a leavening effect on the life of the community.

It is always helpful for residents if the care staff explain what they are doing, and why. Quite often, in a nursing home setting, a carer on a routine task – trimming somebody's toenails or making their bed – may be called away to help with a procedure that needs two people and cannot wait. When that happens, it is helpful to explain to the resident, to give assurance of the speediest possible return, and to apologize for the interruption. In a residential care home or a nursing home, a culture of appreciation and courtesy creates a positive atmosphere that can be felt.

This is not the responsibility of the care workers only; the residents contribute considerably to the forming of relationships of goodwill and affection. In one nursing home where I worked as a night care assistant, everyone enjoyed looking after Hilda. She had left-side paralysis and loss of speech following a stroke, but she had recovered a few words and was able to communicate what she needed us to know, with some guesswork assisting the process. Mostly what she wanted to say was "Thank you" and "I'm so sorry to trouble you". Even when we gave her the wrong thing or did something that didn't work very well for her, she was inclined to be gracious and accepting, sorting things out discreetly once someone who understood her better came along. Hilda had a quiet, retiring nature, but her face had a quality of eagerness and kindness that made us feel welcome as we entered the room. It was a pleasure to be of service to her, and feeding and washing Hilda felt like something of a restorative refuge if the night had been hectic and eventful.

An essential consideration in care work is the matter of setting and maintaining boundaries. Both trust and respect are about boundaries, and for relationships to flourish, clear boundaries must be set.

In a nursing home or residential care home, there is the clear and simple physical boundary of the client's room. This is especially important and helpful where some residents are temporarily confused or suffering from dementia. It is clearly understood that a client's room is their space, into which other residents may enter only by invitation. Residents are usually kind and understanding towards the occasional confused individual wandering in, but this protection of the privacy of the client's space is taken very seriously, because it quickly starts to feel invasive and even frightening if another resident regularly enters without invitation or cannot be disabused of the notion that this is, in fact, his or her bed!

The boundaries of the relationship between resident and carer have to be set and maintained in other ways, and this is of real importance because traditional social boundaries for our interactions with strangers and acquaintances are crossed in the giving of personal care. This is why the carers must be careful in their humour: many residents like to exchange banter, to crack a joke, tease, and be teased, but the career must always err on the side of respect, being mindful to stay within the boundaries appropriate to the relationship, avoiding suggestiveness, mockery, or over-personal observations.

It is also of first importance to remember to greet a resident on entering their room. It is surprisingly easy for a nursing home care assistant in a hurry to become task-focused rather than people-focused, and move directly to the task of changing a pad or putting out clean clothes without remembering to take a moment to make eye contact, smile, say hello, and explain what they have come to do. Especially, it is easy to do this when called to assist someone else – perhaps in lifting and moving a client, or washing a client in bed. Ordering priorities on coming into the room, by greeting first the client and then the other care assistant, does much to affirm the resident as a person and enhance the culture of courtesy and respect. People feel reduced and humiliated if those who perform their care chat over them without including them, or don't bother to talk to them as the procedures are carried out.

One of the ways roles (and therefore also boundaries) are defined in a care setting is in the wearing of uniforms. The doctor, the nursing staff (junior and senior), the care staff, the cleaners, and the kitchen staff will all have distinctive uniforms, usually modelled on hospital styles. These are practical, easy-care clothes without anything that flows or trails. Many people like to keep their work clothes and their home clothes quite distinct, stepping into a professional persona as they dress for work, and so find it helpful to wear a uniform.

Uniforms are also helpful for security. In the UK, everyone working with vulnerable individuals will have had to undergo a Criminal Records Bureau check, so to be given a uniform to wear implies trustworthiness. In a care facility where agency staff often work, the carers may not all be personally acquainted with each other. The uniforms help to identify at a glance that this is someone who is legitimately working here, not a relative who needs help finding a resident or a random interloper off the street.

Uniforms are also a boundary statement in giving personal care, adding relational distance in carrying out intimate procedures, and this helps maintain client dignity.

However, uniforms can be terrifying to some residents, especially if their mental processes are temporarily or permanently confused; carers in uniforms are not infrequently mistaken for police, spies, or the military forces of the enemy. In such cases, it can often be a challenge when the only people available to calm the frightened individual are also wearing uniform. As doctors usually wear their ordinary clothes under their white coats, a doctor who takes off the white coat can be of great help in such a circumstance, especially as medical diagnosis and assistance is likely to be necessary anyway.

Chaplains and chaplaincy volunteers

A chaplaincy team can bring real benefit to a care facility. Nursing homes, especially those which have developed a specialization in palliative care, are likely to have created a formal relationship with ministers of religion in the local area, some of whom may visit all residents who welcome such pastoral contact.

Residential care homes are less likely to have chaplains or regularly visiting ministers of religion, though some do.

Often it is at the initiative of the manager, activities manager, or interested individuals among the care staff that a relationship with a religious body is created, either by residents being supported in attending worship if they are too frail to go alone, or by organizing pastoral visits and opportunities for corporate worship within the care facility itself.

Sometimes the care facility has a religious foundation and continues to be linked to and overseen by a religious denomination, and trustees will include faith representatives who ensure that pastoral and liturgical support and opportunities are offered.

Sharing in an act of worship gives shape to the week, helps to knit the residents together as a community, and is often something that residents look forward to and enjoy.

Ministers of religion will have many responsibilities, and the formation and training of chaplaincy teams for the care facilities in their pastoral area may not make it to the top of the list of their priorities. A chaplain need not be an ordained person, however; there are many lay chaplains.

A small team of volunteers, trained in listening and pastoral visiting, would have much to offer a care facility where the staff may be too few in numbers and too burdened with duties simply to chat for any length of time.

Where residents are alone in the world with no relatives to pop in and see them or bring a bag of sweets or a magazine, a chaplaincy volunteer can fill some of the roles of a friend or relative, offering added stimulus and enrichment to life.

Hermione was a determined and doughty old lady whom I visited regularly as a chaplaincy volunteer over some years. She and I disagreed profoundly about almost everything, but delighted in each other's company and looked forward to our times together very much.

Working as a chaplaincy volunteer, I have been asked to sit with someone recently paralysed by illness who was afraid to be left alone, to take down letters of farewell from a dying lady too weak to write, chat with people whose speech was impaired by illness and for whom conversation needed extra time, or simply spend time with people who otherwise had no visitors. Care staff often willingly go the extra mile with their residents, fetching items from the shop or taking them on outings, but a team of volunteers can offer a welcome additional input.

Chaplains in dark suits and dog-collars, who arrive on the premises holding a Bible and equipped with a clipboard, are less likely to reach a place of real honesty than those who are dressed simply as people. The clerical collar and attire may enable role recognition, but although clerical attire may inspire respect and a set of assumptions about

117

trustworthiness, it will be hard for residents to let down their guard with anyone so formally dressed. A more informal style of dress accompanying the clerical collar helps to signal an approachable, human style, and many clergy now prefer to wear clergy shirts in a colour other than black for pastoral visiting and preaching.

Even so, some people will always feel inhibited in the company of a minister of religion, and chaplaincy volunteers can provide helpfully informal pastoral support.

In the words of the writer Elie Wiesel: "You can't talk to a rabbi, for he is too concerned with relaying your last words to God. You can confess your sins, recite the Psalms or the prayers for the dead, receive his consolation or console him, but you can't talk, not really."

There is tremendous healing in a relationship with someone we can really trust. As the theologian Anthony Padovano said, "In an hour of desperation or loneliness, the voice of the right person can transform us. Even as we die, the voice of someone who meant life for us can assure us we are not lost, we have been heard, we are safe, we shall not die altogether."

The first work in accompanying someone through the great transition from living alone to living in residential care is to establish a relationship of trust. In order to do this, we must have the ability to offer ourselves authentically; to allow ourselves to be seen, as well as ourselves observing and examining; to be ordinary and on the same level, transparently human. The moment we take refuge in a persona or retreat into the shelter of professional status, we have let slip the hand that was holding ours in the dark.

Dr Sheila Cassidy, in her book *Sharing the Darkness*,[5] which came out of her work at St Luke's Hospice in Plymouth, describes in a series of simple line drawings the different possibilities in the ways a patient may relate with their doctor or chaplain.

The first two drawings show the chaplain or medical professional ministering to the patient, supported and equipped with the accoutrements of their profession. The third drawing shows them coming to the meeting without their sacramental vessels or stethoscope, but still bolstered by their skills and professional expertise. The fourth and final picture, of profound encounter, Dr Cassidy describes in these words: "The drawing shows both patient and carers stripped of their resources, presented to each other, naked and empty-handed, as two human beings. There is terrible pain in this impotence, in admitting that one has nothing more to give."

Terrible pain, yes – but also life-giving strength and the foundation for real trust.

Dr Cassidy was writing about a hospice situation, working with people facing the challenges of terminal illness. "Terrible pain" and "impotence" might therefore seem like extreme terminology to make a useful carry-over to the situation of someone who has decided the time has come when it would be more practical to move into a residential care home. Even so, the principles that underlie her observations apply to their situation too – and probably to us all. Imaginatively eroding the potential for "them and us" that could arise from living in a care facility (especially a nursing home) is a contribution the chaplaincy team, the management, and the care staff can between them put in place. It is a question of maintaining, by courtesy and respect, the boundaries that support personal dignity, while developing the empathy and interpersonal skills that facilitate healing encounter.

In addition to a regular programme of outings and events laid on by the activities manager, if there were people with just time to *be* – to sit and chat or be silent, have a cup of tea, knit or read, or just be quietly getting on with something that can be interrupted for a chat – the sense of "home" would be deepened and increased. If the sitting rooms of residential care homes included volunteers dispersed among the residents, working on crosswords together, maybe playing the guitar and singing together, chatting and reminiscing, the tissue of community relationship would develop.

Asking honest questions, chatting together, sharing life, music, coffee, magazines, jokes, and memories – and all without uniforms: this is how trust and friendship begin to form and grow, and how an institution becomes a community – in truth a home.

Pets

By no means all people are animal-lovers, but, for many, home would be incomplete without their pets.

Care homes without animals are easy to find for those who

prefer to live without them, but those homes where pets are included and important make a significant contribution to the well-being of residents who enjoy the companionship of their animal friends.

I took a funeral once for Emma, an old lady who had spent the last year or two of her life in a nursing home, where she was content and felt loved. In describing her situation, her daughter made particular, grateful, mention of the role of a little cat in her mother's last week of life.

The cat, which lived at the nursing home and wandered around freely making friends with everyone, kept Emma company in the days when her life was ebbing away, never leaving her side, curled up close to her on the bed. Both Emma and her daughter derived the deepest comfort from the faithful support and companionship of this little creature.

PAT (Pets As Therapy) dogs and cats also provide a regular therapeutic service to over 100,000 people in care homes, hospital, hospices, special needs schools, and prisons in the UK. Their visits are transformatively healing, often becoming the highlight of the week, and even allowing deeply depressed people to feel they once again have a reason for living.

A loved, temperament-assessed dog or cat can be a real asset in the induction or settling-in period for someone who enjoys the company of animals and finds their presence soothing and helpful.

There are many people of shy or reserved temperament who find it easier to tell their troubles to an animal, and whose souls are nourished by the touch of stroking a pet dog or cat, even though they feel inhibited about touching another human being.

I remember making a bereavement visit to Arthur, a man in his later seventies, following the death of his wife after more than fifty years together. The couple had several small spaniel dogs, whom they loved dearly and who loved them in return. On the occasion of my visit, three of the dogs were curled up together in an armchair, while two were lying on the hearthrug. All were apparently fast asleep.

As we talked, and as he shared with me his memories of his wife and their life together, Arthur began to cry. Immediately, one of the little dogs got up from the hearth rug and went to sit close beside Arthur, the whole length of her body leaning comfortingly against his leg.

I am sure that, although nothing could diminish the sorrow of that loss, having the companionship of his spaniels must have made a profound difference to his experience.

Some care homes, of course, do allow residents to bring their own pets with them, and this, too, provides tremendous comfort and makes the transition much easier.

Resident pets are beneficial to staff and visitors as well as to residents, playing a central part in the development of an ambience of warmth and gentleness, softening the clinical and formal atmospheres created by uniforms and routines.

The twelfth century Abbot Aelred of Rievaulx wrote in his

book *Spiritual Friendship*, "Your friend is the companion of your soul – one to whom you entrust yourself as to another self, one from whom you hide nothing, one from whom you fear nothing." For many people such a relationship, and such a confiding, is possible with an animal where it is not possible with another human being.

Points to remember

• Priorities in choosing a care home are most likely to be locality, staff attitudes, the ambience and environment of the home and grounds, and possibly also any special needs or ideology of the resident.

• Finding ways to help residents continue to express individual choices and preferences, and not robbing them of every measure of independency that is still a practical possibility for them, will enhance their sense of well-being.

• Treating residents with courtesy and respect, and, where possible, arranging their living space to facilitate personal and social (as well as clinical) interactions, restores hope and the sense of being regarded as a human being.

• Trust develops when people get to know one another properly; and well-being cannot flourish without trust. The intimacy of the care relationship promotes trust, and setting clear boundaries also strengthens trust.

- Volunteers may have an important contribution to make here in offering time just to chat and make friends.

- Animals can have a profoundly positive role in promoting well-being, relaxation, comfort, and trust.

CHAPTER 5

Learning to let go begins now

Who goes into residential care? Who would we expect to find living in a residential care home?

If you had a group of people in a seminar and asked them that question, I wonder what answers you would receive.

It seems that when we think about who goes into care, a variety of categories and conditions comes to mind. What those categories have in common is that *they all apply to somebody else*. So, when I (and probably you) think about people living in residential care, there is one thing I am quite clear that they all are: *not me*.

During the time that I was much involved in hospice chaplaincy, I witnessed a curious sequence of events. The staff at the hospice did include one male nurse, but the male employees and volunteers were principally men in middle life and older, in executive roles. Most of the volunteers were older women, and the overwhelming majority of the nursing staff was made up of young and early-middle-aged women.

On the ward at that time was a young woman with motor neurone disease, Marie. Although she coped with it well and her family was tremendously supportive, enabling her to have the best possible quality of life, her slow deterioration was not easy to watch. After a time she went home for a while, as her condition had temporarily stabilized. While she was at home, a new patient came into the hospice: Emily, one of the nurses from among the hospice's own staff. She died there, of cancer. At around the time Emily died, Marie's health deteriorated sharply, and readmittance was sought. After much discussion among the hospice staff, the conclusion was reached that they could not at that time cope with her nursing care. What reason was offered her family, I do not know; the reason given to me was that her care was more than the nursing staff could cope with at that particular moment, coinciding as it did with Emily's recent death – one of their own nurses. Someone like Marie was too close to home: she was too much like them. Watching someone just like themselves die caused such deep trauma that they just couldn't manage a second one until they had been given a little time to recover. It was like watching themselves die, and it was almost too much to bear. In the last days of her life, Marie was cared for in a peaceful side-ward (a single room) in the general hospital. People cannot always handle being reminded that they too will die.

Very often when a person dies from a protracted and difficult disease, loved ones begin a campaign to raise funds and awareness, with the ultimate objective that the day will come when no one ever again suffers and dies from that disease. It is part of the struggle to come to terms with the emotional grief and cost involved in watching the death of somebody you love.

Although the ongoing journey of healing and discovery is a wonderful thing – alleviating suffering, offering hope, and enabling better management and control of diseases for which there is yet no cure – it is important for us to remember that we all have to die of something, and that inherent in the experience of death is the failure of physical systems. This may sound like the science of the obvious – stating nothing more than we already know – but knowledge rests on different levels inside us.

I baptized a baby once for a young woman who never came to church. Curious to know why she sought baptism yet never came to worship, I asked a few questions and learned that the baptism was an expression more of hope than faith. Her own faith had foundered when her grandparents had died. She could not believe God could be so cruel as to take them from her. I enquired the age at which her grandparents had died. She lost her grandfather when he was seventy-six and her grandmother when she was seventy-eight. I thought about this for a minute, then asked her – this sensible young woman old enough to have a child of her own, and with enough initiative to have contacted a minister personally unknown to her – "How long did you think your grandparents would live?" Her answer – honest, heartfelt, childlike, transparent – was: "Oh – for ever!" She was devastated that God had let her down.

But all of us someday will die: everyone we know will die.

No matter how much research is done, how much exercise we take, how careful we are with our diet; even if we drive sensibly and never smoke and only take a glass of wine at Christmas. Even so, we will die, and we do not know when or how. We do not know which of us is quietly developing a silent cancer. Even now the driver may be planning the journey on which his brakes will fail, and my life will be from that day forward in a wheelchair and his will be snuffed out altogether. That embarrassing moment of confusion in the supermarket may be the beginning of Alzheimer's; that silly thing where I somehow tripped over my own foot (how did *that* happen?) the beginning of MS.

This is true for all of us. So far, it is the only thing I have discovered that I can be sure of.

In my early forties, I had just been appointed as minister to a suburban church near London. Through the decades of raising a young family, my greatest fear had been what would happen if I could no longer provide for them. What would happen if their father left me, or died, or was disabled? But that church appointment brought a huge sense of relief. Made it! There we were, with a solid, four-bedroomed house surrounded by a beautiful leafy garden, near the shops and the railway station, safe cycling country, pleasant neighbours. A sense of peace and security swept through me, knowing as I did that almost nothing can dislodge a minister from an appointment. I'd known ministers who couldn't preach, were as pastorally competent as Mr Bean, and couldn't organize their way out of a paper bag, yet were still in post, supported and carried by the patience of loving congregations. Unless I shot the organist or eloped with the chapel steward, now we were finally safe. Within a month the train of events had begun (of which I was blithely unaware) that left me without a job, without a husband, with no idea how to earn a living, and my family without a home. Nothing is certain, nothing lasts for ever, and nobody knows what tomorrow will bring.

Who are the residents in care homes? They are you. They are me. Who goes into residential care? You do. I do.

Although we can do nothing whatsoever to line our future with watertight security, we can do the work on ourselves – the inner work, the soul work – that will enable us to be in our spirits sufficiently supple, spacious, and balanced to integrate and endure whatever experiences lie just around the corner.

And how glad we shall be, incidentally, if we have helped to put into place the best practice, in the residential care homes where we live, that ensures kindness, understanding, and respect, so that those whose circumstances mean they have to live there can find healing, hope, and happiness, instead of the kind of living hell that some care home residents have had to live through.

This inner work makes us ready. Here are some suggestions of what we can be learning and doing right now, so that when frailty, infirmity, and comprehensive loss assail us (and they will), we shall be ready. Unless we die prematurely, we shall all be subject to the ageing process. If we attend to these ten things, we shall be well placed to get the best out of that experience: enhancing our chances of retaining our independence, and our well-being should our independence have to be surrendered.

1 The art of contentment

Today is 3 March, overcast and bitterly cold. The wind is gusting and wild, the rain spattering spitefully across the garden. All is grey, and even now, although it is still late afternoon, the light is fading as if it were only January.

All this week I have been fretful. Everything annoys me. Our two lodgers work different shifts, so I am never alone – and I crave solitude; if I can't be alone most of the time, it drives me crazy. I am trying to get on with some writing, and I share this house with three men. There is no privacy. I get irritable. I become absorbed in what I am doing and forget to start the supper, and my husband comes in saying with the voice of an amazed child, "The recycling bins are still lying around outside!" "Then, bring them in," I say through gritted teeth. There is £131.45 left in my bank account, and this causes me some concern. Furthermore, this house is not where I want to live. I wish I lived in a trailer home, in a narrow boat, or in a small cottage by a field on a hillside, near a stream, near a wood. My family are far away, and I miss them and wish I lived where they do. I miss the light of the ocean. It's getting me down; my soul tugs and pulls at me, wanting to be gone.

I sit in this armchair, thinking, and gradually I start to see things differently. The heating has come on and warmth is seeping through the room: I'm grateful for the warmth.

I have just eaten a luscious pear, exactly the ripeness I like and so juicy – it is a delicious memory in my body. Our Spanish lodger, with his gentle courtesy and his luminous smile, has brought his rent to me early – £350 cash, which is on the floor beside me waiting to be paid in to the bank. From here I have a wonderful view of the garden: at this time of year it is a subtle tapestry of silver greys and cocoa brown and sharp green. The first flowers are coming on the jasmine. I love that shape of the little olive tree, growing outside the window in a terracotta pot, and I like watching the clay sides of the pot dappling with windblown rain. Next to that pot is one of the blue-glazed ones my husband chose; in this moody half-light the colour is so intense and so beautiful. With all that it has and has not, this life is working. If I open my eyes and relax a little, there is so much to appreciate. Contentment is no more than seeing the same things differently; blessing what is there and allowing what is not to rest peaceful.

If the day comes when I must lie or sit quietly and alone in a nursing home room, I hope I will have developed the strength of character to bless the solitude, to delight in the clouds and the birds and squirrels and plants I can see through the window, to savour and remember all that is good; to open my hand in the stream and let all that nags and frets me loosen and flow away.

2 Force of habit
Right now I weigh about thirteen stones (182 pounds or

82.5 kilograms), and this is what I have weighed for some time. Every now and then I make an effort, go on a diet, and shed a few pounds – then I take my eye off the ball, go back to what I always did, and before long I weigh about thirteen stones again. My ideal weight is ten stones (140 pounds or 63.5 kilograms), which is what I weighed when I was a very young woman.

I am coming to terms with the reality that little bursts of effort are not going to make the difference – especially now that I am post-menopausal and my metabolism has slowed down.

If I am going to be a ten-stone woman again, I will have to eat what ten-stone women eat and do what ten-stone women do; not for a little while, but for the rest of my life. If I do that, I shall not have to worry about diets; I shall gradually come into line as a ten-stone woman.

It's what you do all the time, every day, that makes you what you are.

For some years now – about ten years – I have had trouble with my memory. I learned that if I were to fulfil my professional and personal obligations effectively, reliably, and efficiently, I would have to discipline myself to file everything (*now* – not later), to put my keys always in the same place, to apply the handbrake every time I park, to lock the back door every time I close it, to write every agreed date down in my diary immediately. Living like this, I have found the outcome is more satisfactory than that of colleagues and friends with better memories. It helps to have a system. When I forget, when my mind is distracted, when

I am trying to do two things at once, when I am listening to someone as we leave the house, I still put the keys in the right place, lock the back door, file the letters – because now I do it without thinking.

This is what the great Buddhist teacher Thich Nhat Hanh calls "habit energy"; by which he means the momentum that is built up by repeated actions or choices. The repetition creates a protective default mode: habits are very hard to break. The important thing about a habit is that it becomes the thing you do when you are *not* thinking. So if you choose well when you *are* thinking straight, and layer by layer repeat that choice, come the day when you can no longer think straight, that is still the thing you will do.

Creating routines around regular tasks helps to protect our independence for longer. If we always turn the gas off before we lift the pan off the stove, always turn off the light as we leave the room, always put the keys in our pockets before we go out of the front door, always turn off the electrical appliances and close all the doors before we go to bed, we create a safety routine that stands us in good stead. The same is true for routines of cleanliness. To wait until something seems to us to be dirty before we clean it relies too heavily on good eyesight, good memory, and a good sense of smell. At the present time my house-cleaning routines leave much to be desired in this respect, but I know that if I am to create a system that works for my old age, habit will not let me down where observation and memory will.

The force of habit may prolong my years of independence, but if the day comes when I must make the transition to residential care, it will be a great deal easier to do so if I have lived in a systematic manner so that my finances, my papers, and my personal belongings are all up to date and in good order; and my experience in residential care will be easier and happier if I have developed the habits of courtesy and kindness, so that saying "please" and "thank you" with a smile every time and putting others first have become second nature to me – for I will carry on doing it even when my mind has gone.

3 Living simply

To live in simplicity brings a greater freedom and increases the possibilities open to us more than any other single thing we can do. It will empower us more than any other choice we can make.

The less you have, whether in terms of status, possessions, complications, commitments, and wealth, the less can be taken away from you.

To play a part in the community, to enjoy a modest income and the treasure of personal relationships, to have the necessities of everyday living – these are a blessing; but a clutter of belongings, a crammed schedule, a hoard of wealth, and a hectic social life do not create peace or flexibility.

Wise people make enough space in their lives to respond to the unexpected.

Accumulation of possessions in a society based on mass production is a real challenge as we grow older. In the words of the writer Toinette Lippe, "Problems arise when things accumulate."[6] Storing things, cleaning things, finding things, tripping over things, and, above all, loving things – this can become a tyranny.

At some point, as we prepare to make the adjustments that increasing age and declining health will necessitate, we have to grasp the nettle of downsizing. If we create habits of living simply early on in our lives, we will save ourselves much eventual distress. To invest emotionally in the accumulation of possessions robs us of freedom throughout our lives, but never more so than if the time comes to move into residential care.

Probably the most demanding adjustment of all facing people in our society as they move from living in their own homes is coming to terms with a steep and rapid downsizing of possessions.

To reflect and act upon this early in life is the biggest favour we will ever do ourselves.

4 Leaving things behind

Associated with a journey of increasing simplicity is the wise skill of leaving things behind.

If we make this a habit, it will be less hard when the time comes to leave behind the dear familiarity of home.

There are so many things that people can hold on to – injustices done them, opportunities missed, failed relationships, financial loss, grievances, abuses suffered, past experiences of shock or bereavement.

Like Aunt Ada Doom Starkadder (in Stella Gibbons' 1932 novel *Cold Comfort Farm*) whose life was blighted for seventy years because she "saw something nasty in the woodshed", unless we can find the grace to leave things behind and move on, the times of solitude as we grow older will find us haunted by too many ghosts.

I have met a woman in her seventies whose uppermost thought was that her family did not allow her to have piano lessons when she was twelve: this did not make for happiness or for peace of mind.

Sometimes we have to let go of very big things: a marriage that has ended; accepting that we will never have children, or that the children we do have do not love us.

Coming to terms with "what might have been" can also be a hard thing to do. In middle age we may have to face the reality that we shall always be no more than mediocre in our chosen vocation, or that we shall never be rich enough to pursue some particular cherished dream, or that faithfulness to family obligations means a personal ambition can never be realized. Acceptance of what this means can cut very deeply.

It is also important to forgive ourselves for the times we failed and the people we let down, and accept our imperfections and transgressions.

To do the soul work associated with this, even as we are making the journey, will stand us in very good stead. Should the day come when we make the transition to living in residential care, however many outings and entertainments are laid on for us, we shall spend a great deal of time sitting quietly with our thoughts. We shall do ourselves a kindness if we have not hung on to a collection of bitter griefs, guilt, regrets, disappointments, and resentments.

Serenity cannot be achieved until we are willing to leave behind whatever life asks us to put down.

5 Financial provision and preparation

Attitudes to finance vary tremendously, as do the possibilities available to us. But however much or little we have, it should be managed with two possibilities in mind:

a) We may not live to be old.
b) We may live to be old.

Because we may never live to be old, we must remember, as my 81-year-old mother sometimes observes, "There is also such a thing as 'today'".

During the years that I worked in a hospice, I saw several times the bitterness that resulted from people *assuming* they would live to be old. The particular scenario that played itself out over and again was of women who had waited patiently for their hardworking executive husbands to retire. These men had thrown their energies, time, and attention into their work, creating enough wealth to buy a lovely home, a big car, substantial savings. They had paid for their children's needs, paid all their bills, built a conservatory, a deck, a greenhouse, a pergola, a laid brick drive, and a garden shed. Their wives approved of and supported all this, and were waiting patiently for those golden post-retirement years, when their time would come – holidays, cruises, visiting sites of interest, long walks by the sea, in the hills, in the woods. The men reached sixty-five, retired, and died. By far the worst aspect of their widows' grief was the feeling of being utterly cheated – of having snatched away from them the bit they were saving, were so looking forward to; the part that was supposed to be the best bit of all.

We know that we shall die, but we do not know when. It might not even be as late as tomorrow. Even if we do not die for a very long time, we do not know from one day to the next what our state of health may be, or how long we can expect to enjoy use of the faculties we take for granted at the moment. It is important to make time to think about what is really important to us – what we really want to see or do, who we want to spend time with. Is there anywhere we especially want to go? Is there any experience we should be sorry to have missed?

Good financial management includes those things in the budget. Because I walked with my grandson in the Sussex hills, because I breakfasted on the beach with my children, because I gave up the bread-and-butter work and simplified my life to the point where I could afford to devote my days to writing, and because I did what I could to help my children establish themselves in life, I shall have done what I needed to do when the time comes to lay it all down. If my financial management had focused on full-time employment throughout my working years, I would have been responsible in the sense of creating a healthy nest egg, but I would not then have been available to do those things that have been my life's greatest treasure of all.

I may not live to grow old; and there is such a thing as today.

On the other hand, because I may live to be old, I need to have some kind of a plan. What suits individuals will vary, of course, and nobody should make financial decisions without the advice of a person professionally qualified to give such advice (which I am not), but it seems to me that three strategies are likely to be of benefit:

First, do not put all your eggs in one basket. Some secure, long-term, high-interest investments of the usual kinds (bonds, for example); a certain amount of instant-access saving for a rainy day; if possible, some money invested in property; an annuity once old age is upon you and not before (the prices would be too high to be sure of a good return) – such a spread of investment is protective against different contingencies. Investment in collectors' items such as diamonds, gold, or art also creates diversity. It is in the diversity that safety lies. In times such as we are in as I write, when interest rates are as low as can be, to have relied on investment savings is bad news. Those who have bought a little cottage or flat to let out can rely on rents when bank interest is hardly worth having.

There will be many people who consider such advice as being only for the wealthy, yet it is surprising how much we can achieve if we are focused and frugal in our money management. For those who have little or nothing, the problem of choice does not feature; for those who have something put by, it is important to understand that there are pendulum swings, peaks, and troughs – cycles – in every area of life including finance and property. It is diversity in investment that will create stability.

Second, do not leave it too late to pass on what you have to your family. If your children are good people, and you trust them, it is important to pass on to them what you can while you are in good health. It makes sense in any case to downsize gradually; the scenario of one little old lady too frail now for housework or gardening, living alone in a large family house full to bursting with the accumulated clutter of a lifetime, with too small an income to pay tradesmen to keep the property in good repair, blesses nobody and leaves a large legacy of difficult and distressing work.

Do a little research into the cost of residential care. Calculate how quickly it would exhaust your income. Consider now, well ahead of time, what will be the shrewdest use of the funds you have, for yourself and your family. If you are not sure, seek the advice of someone qualified to inform and help you.

One thing in particular that can be done ahead of time is to pay for your funeral. A funeral involves a large number of people and things: a funeral director, four bearers, an officiant, use of a hearse and possibly a limousine and a chapel of rest, maybe an organist, fees for at least one chapel (two if you have a church service followed by a crematorium committal), burial plot fees, fees for crematorium staff. It does not take much reflection to see that, given that each one of the fees relating to each item is increased annually, the yearly increase of the cost of a funeral is staggering.

If you arrange and pay for your funeral in advance, using one of a variety of reputable schemes, not only does it remove a large administrative burden from your family and offer them the comfort of knowing they are carrying out your wishes when you die, but it will save hundreds, probably thousands, of pounds.

Third, do not make yourself too dependent upon the goodwill of others – even the people you love.

In managing your finances, it is both kind and responsible to help and consider your family, but not to the extent of placing yourself unreservedly in their hands. Read *King Lear*. We are not always the best judges of our children's characters, nor of our spouse's.

To so manage your finances that you pass on what you can, while leaving yourself a modest income for your daily needs, reasonable treats, and unforeseen emergencies, while occupying as small a dwelling as is comfortable, is a sensible balance.

6 Counting your blessings

The Christian writer and broadcaster Charles Swindoll said, "We cannot change our past. We cannot change the fact that people will act in a certain way. We cannot change the inevitable. The only thing we can do is play on the one string we have, and that is our attitude."

Many have written about cultivating an "attitude of

gratitude", and pointed out correctly that what we focus on we tend to get more of.

This is not to belittle the everyday difficulties some people live with. I remember working in a nursing home where the routine at midnight included rousing to go to the toilet some residents who did not have to wear incontinence pads, but who could not make it through a full night without a wet bed. One old lady, well into her nineties, comes back to my memory. Roused from profound sleep, it was so hard for her to get out of bed. Her aged joints creaked audibly, and her body was almost too stiff to stand straight or move. It would have been unreasonable and cruel to expect her to be radiating joy.

To perpetuate a false brightness blesses nobody and keeps at arm's length the real help and real relationship that bring real healing to the soul.

Yet it is possible to notice and focus upon what is good and true and positive; to be glad of life's blessings, even when there are many struggles and setbacks.

To focus on the positive in this way can be transformative. Turning from what drags us down and makes us feel angry or depressed, to what makes us laugh, or what we enjoy or makes us happy, can lift our mood and allow us to make something better of the day.

The essential thing is that we grasp, as Swindoll said, that what makes the difference is our *attitude*. As long as we believe that what makes the difference is our *circumstances*, we have given the power over our happiness into the hands of others. Once we grasp that it is attitude, not circumstances, that transforms our experience of life, we have assumed both power and responsibility, and so greatly enhanced our chances of personal happiness.

Counting our blessings also has the valuable effect of shifting our focus of concentration outside ourselves. If I am sitting in my chair feeling grumpy, ill-used, and mortally sorry for myself, but start to count my blessings, I see the beautiful blackbird on the garden deck through the patio door, I taste the ginger biscuit that has come with my cup of tea, and I watch the shadow of leaves thrown against the wall as the sun shines in through the tree in the garden. Awake at night, I hear owls calling to each other, and see the bright moon shining in the frosty sky. The newspaper comes and I have a chance to do the crossword; one of the nurses shows me her engagement ring and stops for a little chat. Each of these things draws me out of the toxic environment of my own misery.

As I count my blessings, each "thank you" I speak is a blessing that feeds my own soul and makes a difference.

7 Appreciating others

Appreciating others has strong connection with counting our blessings, but also warrants a mention of its own.

Black Elk, the famous holy man of the Oglala Lakota, once said, "The power of the world always moves in circles, and everything tries to be round… And so it is with everything where power moves…"

What goes around, comes around: "Cast your bread

upon the waters, and it will return to you after many days"
(Ecclesiastes 11:1).

All people are selfish: it is our animal, biological nature,
the urge of life within us. But some Buddhist teachers have
pointed out that there are wise selfish people and foolish
selfish people. The foolish selfish people put their own
interests above those of others, concentrate on their own
needs and desires, and have no concern for other people.
They generate a society of like-minded souls, in which each
is very vulnerable and alone. Wise selfish people consider
and appreciate others, encouraging them and working for
the well-being of the whole community, and, because they
are part of that community, work in so doing towards their
own well-being, nurture, and security.

The more we expect to be dependent on the mercy and
good nature of others, the wiser it will be to have treated
them with love and appreciation. Since none of us can say
for sure that the day will never come when we shall be
dependent on others for assistance in our everyday care,
it is probably a good idea to start now to create habits of
appreciation, courtesy, and kindness. Even should we
remain independent to our dying day, it seems unlikely we
should regret the formation of those habits.

8 Asking

In his beautiful meditation *Desiderata*, Max Ehrmann says,
"You are a child of the universe, no less than the trees and
the stars; you have a right to be here." This is a profound

and important truth, and it means that we are right to speak up for ourselves – not to whinge and grumble, but to say what we need, what would make us happy, if we are uncomfortable or sad or afraid.

We should not be afraid or embarrassed to say what is important to us. Some of us may have been brought up in a culture where to state one's own needs and preferences was thought to be selfish; sacrificing oneself for others may have been the aspirational norm, but in fact this tends to build unhealthy relationships fraught with misunderstandings. We hope the others will notice and anticipate our needs as we (think we) have noticed and anticipated theirs, but even if they love us, they may not be so good at second-guessing what will make us happy. It is a relief to everyone if we ask, if we say, if we explain, if we are honest – not rude or provocative or complaining, just honest.

9 Living in the light of something greater than yourself

I believe that one of the best recipes for vitality that goes beyond simple health and strength is living in the light of something greater than ourselves.

Those who believe in a Higher Being, in Holy Spirit, or those who feel a sense of purpose to their lives, who see themselves as working for a cause that really matters, as channelling divine power and resting on divine grace, draw down tremendous strength through that faith.

The difficulty is, of course, that it's hard to believe

something on purpose – you can't *make* yourself think something is true; you can't select "religious faith" for your shopping basket, press "submit", and sit back to wait for it to be delivered.

Even so, it is possible to give your soul a chance, to develop curiosity about what lies beyond you, becoming informed about the lives and faiths of others. We might ask about where our food comes from and what is the effect of different agricultural approaches, how our cosmetics are tested, about the political structures of our society, about how and where our savings are invested. We might look around us and ask *why* that child is so out of control, how that man came to be an alcoholic passed out on a public bench, what the history is of that homeless Roma woman begging on the street corner.

As we look beyond our own personal daily concerns, we may awaken an interest, even a passion, in working to right what is wrong, to make human society more just, to create hope, to leave this world more beautiful than we found it.

Drawn into what fires our passion, we find ourselves living in the light of something greater than ourselves – and this energizes us. Our ailments and anxieties fade into the background, physical discomfort is lessened, our worries and grudges are minimized – because we are thinking about something else.

Faith in God is rightly described as a gift. So it is: faith is a pearl of great price; but faith in almost anything greater than oneself is a release from the fetid environment of a stagnant inner world where nothing is allowed in except what was already there in the beginning.

To leave home and make the transition to residential care is not easy for anybody, but it is made easier when the focus of one's thoughts is determined by a cause more pressing than one's memories, house, and possessions.

10 The one we don't want to think about

The diabetes statistics in the US and UK give cause for grave concern – perhaps especially in the UK because of the extremely steep increase gradient.

We have to eat well and get moving.

During the time I was a pastor on the outskirts of London, my congregations lived just over ten miles away from London Bridge, in the heart of the capital. We had a remarkable number of very spry elderly people in those congregations – in one of them, eight women were over ninety. As I visited them in their homes and listened to their reminiscences, what I noticed particularly was how much walking they had done in earlier years. They thought nothing, back then, of walking in to Methodist Central Hall in Westminster (in central London) for evening service. Leisure activities were picnics or gathering blackberries on Hayes Common. It seemed that almost everything they did happened several miles away from where they started – and, in those days, none of them had cars.

As middle age assailed me and the Battle of the Bulge began, one of my daughters (then in her mid-teens) remarked, "The reason middle-aged people aren't as slim as teenagers is that they don't live like teenagers – they go everywhere in cars." This observation has stayed with me, and, however much I turn it round, I can't find anything wrong with it.

Everyone, even the most athletic, has to grow old, and good diet and plenty of exercise ensure neither longevity nor good health. My second husband, Bernard, whose idea of an afternoon of fun was a thirteen-mile hike across the Ashdown Forest, and who'd been eating muesli before anyone else even knew how to spell it, died of kidney cancer and a horrible autoimmune disease. His previous wife was as slender as a willow wand and spent her days working in the garden, doing her own and several other people's housework, and walking in the hills and woods of Sussex in pursuit of her vocation as a landscape painter. She died of breast cancer a little way into her sixties. There are no guaranteed rewards. Each of us knows one legendary old granny who smokes like a chimney, lives on meat pies and custard creams, and only walks as far as the kerbside – but only one.

Once past the menopause, my body nosedived. Pain in all my tissues kept me awake at night, acid reflux came searing up my gullet after every meal and snack, I felt stiff and inflexible, tired and low in spirits, and my weight was increasing inexorably. Writing is a sedentary occupation, I loathe sports, dislike communal settings (for example, the gym) and would prefer not to go out jogging along the (very) public highway, and very low calorie regimes tip me

148

into depression. And then I discovered Wii Fit. The pounds have rolled off, I feel alive and energized, my work output has increased amazingly, I feel twenty years younger – and all this is achieved in the privacy of my own living room, far away from the patronizing gaze of muscle-bound gym bunnies. The TV exercise guru Mr Motivator used to say, "To make the body move, you gotta let the body groove", and I think that is probably the key to success. Nobody does what they aren't enjoying for very long.

When I go to visit my mother and sister, I look forward to a slice of cake (or two or three). I like to add a little chocolate cereal to my low calorie flake, bran sticks, and unsweetened soya milk of a morning. I am not into self-denial, and I do not tell myself I can't have anything. On the other hand, there are certain things I make sure have been on my lunch plate – lots and lots of vegetables, with the green leafy ones strongly represented. I buy very lean meat, dividing the contents of the pack and putting some in the freezer, I go easy on eggs, eat almost no hard cheese, and am very frugal indeed with the soft cheese and the butter. I like brown rice but eat very little bread or pasta. I snack on fruit, with a plain biscuit to accompany a mid-afternoon cup of tea. My mother, who is in her eighties, follows a similar pattern. She doesn't have a Wii Fit, but she is a keen gardener and makes sure to do her grocery shopping little by little every day, so she always has a reason to walk right across town to the store. She hasn't even a hint of diabetes, though her brother and her sister who love the scones and the sherry both struggle with it.

149

I accept that the day may come when I have to live in residential care – like my friend Margery who was lean, fit, and active, but who in her closing years suffered from blindness and memory loss that made it dangerous for her to continue living alone – but observation, common sense, and personal experience all convince me that my diet and exercise level are overwhelmingly likely to have a very significant influence on my quality of life as I age, and that remains true even if I develop life-limiting illness.

In a book about helping people make the transition from living in their own homes to living in residential care, it may seem that such reflections come too late. This is because our society is in general afflicted with a short-termism that hinders us from seeing the bigger picture.

We can become addicted to the opinions of experts and compliant with the dominion of authority, distrusting our own intuition sometimes to the extent of ignoring the evidence of our own eyes.

As I reflect more deeply, I realize that many life events, represented as discrete event segments, in fact ramify more deeply and widely into our experience and are present with us more diffusely than first appears.

If you do a little research on the average length of labour in giving birth to a child, you will come up with varying results: perhaps that twelve to fourteen hours is about normal, and thirty-eight hours is long but becoming more normal. On the basis of my own observation as the mother of five children and in what I have noticed in goats, sheep, dogs, and cats giving birth, I would say that birth takes place over many days: that a labour is like a tide flowing over a week, maybe two. It is the part that comes to the attention of the doctor, the midwife, or the vet that is charted – and that becomes therefore definitive of what a labour "is".

Similarly with our questions about how long it takes to die, how long is the course of a disease such as Alzheimer's, or what is a good standard of care, it is in the nature of things that answers are given from the viewpoint of carers and professionals – until someone diagnoses and records, it isn't happening.

Part of the task of developing wisdom is to deepen and increase sensitivity to the tides of life: the wind and sea currents of the soul, the breathing and heartbeat of human reality, learning patience, and gradually releasing fear. This takes time.

If we come at this issue of when to make the transition from independence to residential care from the perspective of a social worker, a chaplain, a relative, or a care assistant, we come up with a variety of answers: when the individual can no longer cope without supervision; if there is severe memory or mobility impairment perhaps; when the person's relatives can no longer manage to give the necessary care; when someone becomes a danger to themselves.

But if we come at the issue from the perspective of human wisdom, we recognize that our transit through this life is a seamless learning curve in which we are always passing into new experiences of reality, impermanence, and release. We come to realize that the transition is from life to death, from death to life, and is happening all the time. So when we wonder about the right moment to get ready to make this transition, when to begin the difficult process of learning to let go, we begin to realize that the only feasible answer has to be "now"; and the sooner, the better.

Neither I writing this, nor you reading it, can possibly begin to conjecture what will happen to us tomorrow or tonight, but we can know with certitude that if we have begun to learn the wisdom of learning to let go, we shall be better prepared for anything that presents at any time, and we will be wiser and more supportive companions for those who are struggling to cling, for whom life is torn from them because they cannot bring themselves to let go.

I feel embarrassed to be giving you advice. What you must do is what you can do, and I cannot tell you what that is. But I do venture this: give yourself time. In your every day, make margins. Build a central reservation and a soft shoulder to plough into in case the wheels come off as you are hurtling along. Give yourself time with the people you love. Give yourself time to look at the clouds and the sea, and listen to the soughing of great trees in the night wind. Give yourself time to listen to music and watch films and walk in the woods and enjoy relaxed meals with your friends. Give yourself time to adventure and discover, time to get to know your children, time to make friends with animals, time to bend down and look at the face of a flower, time to watch ants construct their kingdoms. Give yourself time to find out what it was you came here to do, and time to do that. Give yourself time in silence, time to reach out into the unknown and touch the face of God. If you give yourself time to really live and really love, then, when it is time, I think you will be able to let go.

May God bless your journey.

Points to remember

• An important step in attaining wise maturity is accepting that we ourselves may one day be the people making the transition into residential care. Looking honestly at this reality encourages us to open our minds to the changes and attitudes that will benefit us for the whole of our life journey.

• Accepting impermanence and mortality enables us to order our priorities so as to live without regrets.

• We cannot control or predict what unforeseen events may overtake us, but we can foster the attitudes that will equip us to meet them with strength and equilibrium.

• Contentment is found in choosing to look for the positive.

• It is important to make wise choices in laying down our habits, for they carry us along on their momentum.

• Living simply increases freedom, flexibility, and choice.

• Serenity depends on our willingness to let go of what life is taking out of our hands.

• Wise management of our finances involves maintaining

the balance of living rich and full lives now, while planning some provision for the future.

• Consciously developing an "attitude of gratitude" will greatly increase our well-being.

• Treating others with appreciation is a wise investment that pays dividends.

• Courteously but clearly speaking up and stating our own needs is helpful and has a better likely outcome than waiting until somebody notices.

• Looking beyond our own personal daily concerns, discovering a meta-narrative that will offer a context for our lives, provides comfort, inspiration, and strength.

• Responsible attention to diet and exercise can beneficially transform our experience of ageing.

• The tides of life turn slowly. It is never too early to develop the attitudes and habits that will stand us in good stead for our future. Give yourself the gift of time.

Notes

1. For details of this research go to: http://www.lancashire.
gov.uk/corporate/news/press_relcases/y/m/release.
asp?id=200712&r=PR07/0672
For more information call 01772 530098 or visit online at:
www.lancashire.gov.uk/telecare
2. Sheffield (UK) Council website includes an excellent list
of questions to ask in choosing the right care home, at the
following link: http://www.sheffield.gov.uk/safe--sound/
social-services/getting-help-from-social-services/help-for-
adults/residentialandnursingcare/questionstoask
3. *Library of Nations: India*, Time-Life Books BV, 1986.
4. W. David Wills, *Spare The Child*, London: Penguin,
1971. Now out of print, but second-hand copies can be
obtained online.
5. Sheila Cassidy, *Sharing the Darkness: The Spirituality of
Caring*, London: Darton, Longman & Todd, 1988.
6. Toinette Lippe, *Caught in the Act*, New York, NY: Jeremy
P. Tarcher/Penguin, 2004, p. 26.

Appendix of useful contacts and starting points

The following list of organizations is not exhaustive. All information is correct at the time of printing.

UK

Age UK was created in April 2010 from a merger of Age Concern and Help the Aged. This charity plays an important role in supporting and promoting the well-being of all older people, helping them to make later life a fulfilling and enjoyable experience.
www.ageuk.org
Tel: 0800 107 8977

The Alzheimer's Society is committed to maintaining, improving, and promoting its unique knowledge and understanding of dementia.
www.alzheimers.org.uk
Helpline: 0845 300 0336
Tel: 020 7423 3500

Carers UK is the voice of carers who look after family, partners, or friends in need of help because they are ill, frail, or have a disability. Carers UK is the only care-led organization working for all carers.
www.carersuk.org
Helpline: 0808 808 7777
Tel: 020 7378 4999

The Care Quality Commission is an independent regulator of health and social care. Its aim is to ensure that better care is provided for everyone, in hospital, care homes, people's own homes, or elsewhere. It regulates health and adult social care services, whether provided by the NHS, local authorities, private companies, or voluntary organizations.
www.cqc.org.uk
Tel: 03000 616161

Counsel and Care provides advice and help for older people. Counsel and Care's advice work team works over the telephone and by letter backed up by a range of well-researched and regularly updated fact sheets. It is able to advise on a wide range of subjects such as welfare benefits, accommodation, residential care, community care, and hospital discharge.
www.counselandcare.org.uk
Advice line: 0845 300 7585
Tel: 020 7241 8555

The Registered Nursing Home Association provides information for nursing home owners and staff, for people seeking a nursing home place, and for members of the public with an interest in the care of older people and those with disabilities.
www.rnha.co.uk
Tel: 0121 451 1088

USA

The AGS Foundation for Health in Aging is a national non-profit organization that aims to build a bridge between the research and practice of geriatrics and the public, and to advocate on behalf of older adults and their special health care needs.
www.healthinaging.org
Toll free: (800) 563 4916
Tel: (212) 755 6810

The Alzheimer's Association is a leading voluntary health organization in Alzheimer care, support, and research. It aims to eliminate Alzheimer's disease through the advancement of research, to provide and enhance care and support for all affected, and to reduce the risk of dementia through the promotion of brain health.
www.alz.org
Helpline: (800) 272 3900

The Consumer Consortium on Assisted Living is a national non-profit consumer-based organization that

focuses on the needs, rights, and protection of assisted-living consumers, their caregivers, and loved ones.
www.ccal.org
Tel: (703) 533 8121

LongTermCareLiving.com is sponsored by the American Health Care Association and the National Center for Assisted Living. It provides consumers with information about nursing homes, assisted living/residential care, and other types of long-term care.
www.longtermcareliving.com
Tel: (202) 842 4444
They also offer a **glossary** of care terms: www.longtermcareliving.com/glossary/

MemberoftheFamily.net provides information about 16,000 Medicare/Medicaid-certified nursing homes in the United States, including easy-to-understand reports based on recent government surveys. It also compiles a National Watch List of homes recently cited for violations or substantiated complaints, and an Honor Roll of facilities found to be deficiency-free.
www.memberofthefamily.net